☶ INSIGHT COMPACT GUIDE

Greece

Compact Guide: Greece is the ultimate quick-reference guide to this fascinating destination. It tells you all you need to know about Greece's attractions, from its mountains and beaches to its churches and archaeological sites, not forgetting its culture and food, and its lively and historic capital, Athens.

This is one of 133 Compact Guides, which combine the interests and enthusiasms of two of the world's best known information providers: Insight Guides, whose titles have set the standard for visual travel guides since 1970, and Discovery Channel, the world's premier source

Insight Compact Guide: Greece

Written by: Claudia Christoffel-Crispin and Gerhard Crispin
English version by: Paul Fletcher
Updated by: Marc Dubin
Photography by: Phil Wood
Additional Photography by: Pete Bennett, Nick Bonnetti, Guglielmo Galvin, Glyn Genin, Anna Mockford, Bill Wassman and Gregory Wrona
Cover picture by: Gregory Wrona
Picture Editor: Hilary Genin
Maps: Polyglott

Editorial Director: Brian Bell
Managing Editor: Tony Halliday

CONTACTING THE EDITORS: As every effort is made to provide accurate information in this publication, we would appreciate it if readers would call our attention to any errors and omissions by contacting:
Apa Publications, PO Box 7910, London SE1 1WE, England.
Fax: (44 20) 7403 0290
e-mail: insight@apaguide.co.uk

Information has been obtained from sources believed to be reliable, but its accuracy and completeness, and the opinions based thereon, are not guaranteed.

© 2005 APA Publications GmbH & Co. Verlag KG Singapore Branch, Singapore.

First Edition 2002; updated 2005
Printed in Singapore by Insight Print Services (Pte) Ltd
Original edition © Polyglott-Verlag Dr Bolte KG, Munich

Worldwide distribution enquiries:
APA Publications GmbH & Co. Verlag KG (Singapore Branch)
38 Joo Koon Road, Singapore 628990
Tel: (65) 6865-1600, Fax: (65) 6861-6438

Distributed in the UK & Ireland by:
GeoCenter International Ltd
The Viables Centre, Harrow Way, Basingstoke,
Hampshire RG22 4BJ
Tel: (44 1256) 817987, Fax: (44 1256) 817988

Distributed in the United States by:
Langenscheidt Publishers, Inc.
36–36 33rd Street 4th Floor, Long Island City, NY 11106
Tel: (1 718) 784-0055, Fax: (1 718) 784-0640

www.insightguides.com

Introduction

Places

Culture

Travel Tips

△ **Mystrás (p49)**
This wonderfully preserved and deserted Byzantine city was a bastion of Orthodox culture. Its churches house superb religious frescoes.

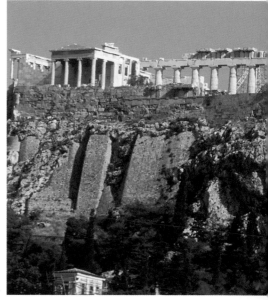

△ **The Acropolis (p26)**
One of the most famous archaeological sites in the world, Athens' Acropolis boasts the architectural masterpiece of the Parthenon, the exquisite Temple of Athena Nike and the huge Roman Odeon.

△ **Thessaloníki (p70)**
Greece's second city is noted for its Byzantine remains, excellent food and elegant shopping streets.

▷ **Mycenae (p42)**
Steeped in history, this spectacular site has the famous Lion Gate, cyclopean walls and 'beehive' tombs.

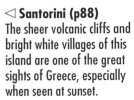

◁ **Santorini (p88)**
The sheer volcanic cliffs and bright white villages of this island are one of the great sights of Greece, especially when seen at sunset.

▷ **Knossos (p96)**
The reconstruction of this fascinating Minoan palace evokes the life and culture of this ancient civilisation.

Crete's beaches (p94)
me of Greece's best
aches are found on Crete,
om the shallow waters of
afonísi, to secluded Préveli.

Delphi (p56)
e centre of the ancient
orld is set against the
riking backdrop of Mount
irnassós.

▽ **Rhodes Town (p90)**
The winding alleys and fortifications of the Crusaders give Rhodes a medieval feel, while the lively Mandráki harbour was the site of the famous Colossus.

△ **Metéora (p60)**
The spectacular perched monasteries of Metéora cling to the heights of precipitous rocks overlooking the Thessalian plain. The monastery interiors are richly decorated with beautiful frescoes and icons.

Cradle of Europe

Greece is easy to fall in love with. Mountains and villages, beaches and temples lie bathed in the famously clear Aegean light. The people of this radiant country are open, intelligent and passionate. Many travellers first experience these qualities in the warm welcome given them, and these same travellers return time after time – for the mirror-smooth Aegean Sea shimmering in the still of the morning, for the *kafenía* with their wooden chairs and rickety tables offering some shade from the blistering afternoon heat, and for the silvery-green olive groves where cicadas trill until evening. In addition, Greece's self-evident physical beauty is complemented by some of the most important and stunning archaeological sites in Europe.

Opposite: Dodona, Epirus
Below: Ásos, Kefalloniá

LOCATION AND SIZE

Stretching across the tip of the Balkan Peninsula from the Ionian Sea to the Aegean, Greece stands at one corner of Europe, and has always served as a bridge to Asia. Neighbours include Turkey, Bulgaria, the former Yugoslav republic of Macedonia, and Albania. But despite its geographical remoteness, ties with western Europe were strengthened by Greece's accession to the EEC in 1981. Islands make up one-fifth of the total surface area of 131,986 sq km (50,960 sq miles), with Gávdos, an islet off Crete, marking the southernmost point of Europe.

The physical geography of the country is characterised by deep valleys, furrowed mountain ranges and a jagged, generally rocky coastline. Even beneath the surface confusion reigns, as the country lies above a tectonically active region of the earth's crust, making earthquakes a fairly frequent phenomenon. Flat, fertile areas such as the Thessalian plain are the exception rather than the rule. Large parts of the country suffer from drought despite regular rainfall, usually between October and April.

MOUNTAINS, COAST AND ISLANDS

Mainland Greece is made up of Attica, the Peloponnese, Roumeli, Thessaly, Epirus, Macedonia and Thrace. The extensive Píndos mountain range in the west forms the country's backbone, while in the east the peak of Mount Olympus at 2,917m (9,570ft) is the highest in Greece.

The convoluted coastline forms so many coves and inlets that it runs to a length of 15,000 km (9,320 miles). The hundreds of islands that spill out into the seas surrounding Greece are divided into a number of distinct groups: the Ionian islands to the west, the Sporades to the east, the east Aegean islands and Dodecanese off the coast of Turkey, and the Cyclades trailing southeast from Athens. Crete and Rhodes are two of the largest islands; both of them are famous for their variety of flowers, although the flora throughout Greece is remarkable.

CLIMATE

Lovers of nature and walkers will find April and May, when the wildflowers are in full bloom and the countryside is sweetly scented, the best time of year to visit Greece. During June, in shallow waters and in the south, water temperatures can be comfortable for bathers. July and August can see the thermometer rising to 45°C (113°F) in southern and central Greece. In the Aegean and in particular along the north coast of Crete the strong northerly *meltémi* winds brings some relief from the sweltering heat of high summer. Many visitors to Greece prefer September when the sea is still warm and the tourist influx has waned, but from the middle of October it can turn quite cool and rain can be frequent. From then until March, Greece is only for the hardened traveller, olive harvester or winter-sports fan. Few hotels are open and even then only a handful, on the islands at least, are equipped for winter weather. However, there are a few advantages: the major sites are almost deserted, the winter sun is more reliable than in northern Europe, and Athens and Thessaloníki are at their best without the stifling heat and crowds of tourists.

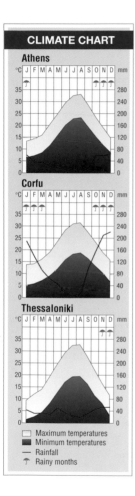

CLIMATE CHART

Athens

Corfu

Thessaloníki

☐ Maximum temperatures
■ Minimum temperatures
— Rainfall
☂ Rainy months

NATURE AND THE ENVIRONMENT

Blossom smothers the almond and lemon trees, flowering meadows are shaded by olive trees, cicadas hum and the scent of thyme wafts through the clear air. With such an idyllic setting, humans and nature seem to live in perfect harmony. However, this does not bear close examination.

Ancient and medieval shipbuilders cut down the original trees, then second growth was cut for firewood and to clear fields for growing cereals, and now land speculators set fire to the remaining coniferous forests. Dry soil and hungry goats prevent regrowth. Happily, there is still the olive. In sparse scrubland, where scarcely any water is to be found for miles around, a gnarled olive tree will still manage to grow, with goats and sheep letting its leaves well alone.

The mountain regions in the north are a different world. Brown bears, wolves and wild cats roam the Víkos-Aóös and Píndos National Parks *(see pages 65 and 63)*. But nature reserves in the Néstos and Ahelóös deltas are threatened by hydro-electric power stations and dams.

The damage has already been done to the Aegean Sea. Although still relatively clean, it has been severely overfished. Greece has the longest coastline in Europe, but the fewest fish, so many of the old fishing villages now rely on catching tourists. The delicious grilled fish served in the

Forest fires
Perhaps the greatest threat to Greece's environment are the summer forest fires that consume more of its precious woodland every year. These are blamed variously on carelessly discarded matches or bottles, but usually on arson. Once the forests have been burnt, unscrupulous developers move in to start building. The government has been attacked for relaxing the rules on encroachment on protected land, thus encouraging further destruction. Areas that have recently seen devastating fires include Mount Olympus, Mount Párnitha and the islands of Thássos, Kárpathos and Sámos.

A wooded landscape, Kefalloniá

harbour tavarnas may have originated in the Atlantic. In the easternmost Sporades islands, environmentalists have established a marine nature reserve, primarily for the preservation of the endangered Mediterranean monk seal.

The Goulandris Natural History Museum, at Levídou 13 in the Athens suburb of Kifissiá, gives a good summary of Greek flora and geology.

Environmental issues do not yet play an important enough role in routine Greek politics. Problems caused by industrial waste or agricultural practices are often ignored. The smog (*néfos* in Greek), is causing considerable damage to many of Athens' treasures, but controls on traffic emissions – and the new metro – are slowly improving the air in Athens. One of the major causes of pollution is mass tourism, which has prompted the construction of poorly conceived hotels without the proper infrastructure to support them.

Below: a face of modern Greece
Bottom: Athens' sprawl

POPULATION

Two-thirds of the 10.5 million inhabitants of the Ellinikí Dimokratía, Greece's official title, live in eight major cities, with approximately four million in the Greater Athens area and one million in Thessaloníki. There are small indigenous Muslim, Catholic, evangelical and Jewish minorities, but the most important demographic factor in

recent years is a huge immigrant population of well over a million, the vast majority Albanian.

Before the arrival of these foreigners, the most crucial pattern in Greece was a massive population movement from the countryside to the towns. Athens and Thessaloníki, offering better job prospects and a higher standard of living, become the destinations of most former village-dwellers, but every provincial capital acted like a magnet for its hinterland. On the islands and rural mainland regions, only tourism can offer local people a viable living, in the retailing, catering or service trades. That comes hard in a country where, traditionally, most people like to be the 'boss' or else work for the state. Some 40 percent of Greeks are still self-employed.

Emigration has also been a fact of life for many Greek families. Over three million live abroad, with Australia's Melbourne, home now to 500,000 Greeks, sometimes described as Greece's third-biggest city.

Since 1991 more than 10 million tourists have visited the country in a good year, although numbers have flagged since the millennium, as price-hikes have made Greece less competitive. Most tourists are given a cordial welcome; the Greek word *xénos*, the honourable name for a visitor, means not only 'stranger' but also 'guest'.

RELIGION AND CUSTOMS

Over 90 percent of the population belong to the Greek Orthodox Church, which long played a central role in everyday life. Religious faith and Greek nationality were inseparable for generations, civil marriages were not introduced until 1982 and symbols demonstrating the importance of the people's religious belief can be seen everywhere. The recent controversy over the removal of a person's religion from Greek identity cards (in line with EU policy) pointed up the close correlation between 'Greekness' and Orthodoxy. No village is without a church, and small shrines are dotted along virtually all rural roads. These shrines or *proskinitária*, sometimes in the form

Easter traditions

Easter is the major festival of the Greek Orthodox Church. The *epitáfios* (the grave and shroud of Christ) procession takes place on Good Friday evening. Lambs are slaughtered and *mayerítsa*, a soup made from lamb offal, is cooked on Saturday evening. Just before midnight, the priest turns out the church lights, the Easter candles in front of the altar are lit and the flame is then passed from one candle to another among the congregation. People return home, carefully keeping their candles lit, and a cross is marked on the front door lintel with candle soot, after which they eat. The traditional greeting is *Hristós anésti* (Christ is risen), to which the reply is *alithós anósti* (truly he is risen). Red-painted Easter eggs are knocked together and the person whose egg survives longest is considered lucky.

Church interior, Zákynthos

Athens' Central Market

of miniature churches, either serve as substitutes for more remote chapels dedicated to the same saint, or as memorials for road accidents.

POLITICS

The word 'politics' derives from the Greek *téhni politikí* meaning 'the art of governing'. The current Greek constitution was adopted in 1975, following the collapse of the colonels' junta and deposition of the royal family. This established a parliamentary republic, with a president as head of state. The parliament has a single chamber with 300 elected members, led by the prime minister.

Elections held in March 2004 brought the conservative ND (Néa Demokratía, or New Democracy) party to power by a convincing margin over PASOK (Panhellenic Socialist Movement), which had governed for 20 of the previous 23 years, first with Andreas Papandreou as prime minister, and later under Kóstas Simitis. The present government is led by Kóstas Karamanlís, nephew of the late Konstantínos Karamanlís, the party's founder and former prime minister and president. The current president of Greece, mostly a figurehead position, is Konstantínos Stefanópoulos.

The only other parties with MPs in the current parliament are the KKE (old-style communists, reinvented as an anti-EU, anti-globalisation movement), and the Synaspismós (Coalition of the left), broadly Euro-communist and more sympathetic to the goals of the EU. An extreme right-wing Orthodox Christian party, LAOS, has a single representative in the European Parliament.

ECONOMY

Although the Greek economy has long ranked with Portugal's at the bottom of the European league, there are hopeful signs. Inflation has dropped to single figures, interest rates are down to near the continental European norm, and only the vast overspending on the 2004 summer Olympics pushed the national debt over the 3 percent of GDP limit imposed by the EU. Greece is in fact poised to become a major Balkan economic power, with Greek businesses the principal or second investors in Bulgaria, Albania, Serbia and Romania, plus increasing investments in Turkey.

Wages don't always keep pace with inflation and strikes may cause disruption. Many workers supplement their income with second jobs – the 'black' cash economy is estimated to account for over a third of transactions. The number of unfinished buildings demonstrate how people quickly run out of money. Even with massive EU subsidies, Greek farmers have difficulty competing against European agribusinesses; landholdings are small and farmed with resolutely traditional methods. The main export products are citrus fruits and olive oil from its more than 120 million olive trees; Greek oil production ranks third in the EU behind Spain and Italy. But only a quarter of the working population is employed in agriculture, and the merchant marine is in decline; by far the largest enterprise is tourism, along with allied service trades. Balance of payments remains a problem: the value of imports such as cars, electrical goods and exotic foodstuffs exceeds the value of exports (clothes, wine, fruit, vegetables, tobacco and cotton) by more than half. Much of the formerly obsolete infrastructure was greatly improved in the run-up to the 2004 Olympics, with massive aid from the European Investment Bank.

Agriculture and shipping: two of Greece's major industries

A Potted History

One of the earliest civilisations to have arisen in Greece was the Minoan civilisation of Crete (c. 3000BC–1100BC). Its name derives from Minos, either a dynastic title or the name of a legendary ruler. The Minoans developed the island into a flourishing trading centre, built remarkable cities and palaces, and produced beautiful works of art.

Below: a Bronze Age Cycladic figure
Bottom: the Minoan palace, Agía Triáda, Crete

THE MYCENEANS AND DORIANS

The Myceneans from mainland Greece had little difficulty in conquering the unfortified cities of the Minoans. In the 14th century BC the Myceneans built fortifications to defend their Peloponnesian citadels at Mycenae and Tiryns against the Dorian invaders from northern Greece. However, by 1200BC the Dorians had overrun large areas of the Peloponnese, and the Ionian and the Aeolian tribes had settled in Attica, on the island of Évvia and along the coast of Turkey.

It was the Olympian gods of the Dorians that became the dominant pantheon of Greece, supplanting the Minoan and Mycenean deities. There were seasonal festivals and religious celebrations, the most famous of which were the quadrennial Olympic Games, first verifiably held in 776BC, in honour of Zeus and Hera.

THE ARCHAIC PERIOD

The 8th century BC onwards saw the creation of the city-states, the most powerful of which were Athens, Sparta, Thebes, Corinth and Argos. Population growth led to expansion, and colonists established new Greek cities in Asia Minor and along the Black Sea, as well as today's France, Spain and North Africa. In the Peloponnese, Sparta become a powerful military force. In 550BC, to consolidate its position, Sparta formed the Peloponnesian League with neighbouring city-states. Their rival, Athens, became a leading centre for the arts and philosophy.

THE CLASSICAL PERIOD

The 5th and 4th centuries BC saw intense power struggles and years of conflict, particularly against the Persians *(see margin box)*. After the final defeat of the Persians in 479BC, Athens formed the Attic Naval League. Ionian and Aeolian coastal towns joined forces with Athens in order to deter another Persian assault. The confederacy, based on Delos, was dominated by Athens, but was seen by the Spartans as a challenge to their supremacy, particularly when the treasury was transferred to Athens in 454BC.

Athens became involved in a dispute with Corinth, a member of the Peloponnesian League; this was the catalyst for the Peloponnesian Wars (431–404BC), with Sparta and Athens as the main protagonists. In 404BC Athens was captured and the Attic Naval League disbanded. Sparta now controlled a large part of Greece, but a Spartan raid on Thebes in 382BC was repulsed; the Peloponnesian League began to disintegrate, and Sparta's power declined. Athens again became pre-eminent in Greek cultural life.

THE HELLENISTIC PERIOD

The return of Athenian power was halted by Philip II of Macedonia whose victory in the battle of Chaeronea (338BC), brought all the Greek cities but Sparta under Macedonian rule. Philip

Persian invasions

In 490BC the Persian king, Darius, was intent on conquering Greece. However, his soldiers were defeated at Marathon, 42km (26 miles) northeast of Athens, by the Athenian general Miltiades. In 480BC Xerxes, the son of Darius, invaded once more. But the city states formed themselves into an alliance. The Spartan king Leonidas was defeated at Thermopylae Pass, 20km (12 miles) south of modern Lamía. However, the Greeks won naval battles off the islands of Salamis and Sámos. The final land defeat of the Persians was at the Battle of Plataea in Boeotia in 479BC.

Classical relief in the National Museum

Byzantine icon, Ekatondapylianí, Páros

was assassinated in 336BC and succeeded by his son, Alexander the Great, who briefly made Macedonia into a world power.

Alexander's aim was to create an empire that would unite Greeks and Persians. When he died in 323BC this vast empire was carved up by his generals, whose dynastic rule lasted until the Romans arrived. By the end of the 3rd century BC, Rome had begun to emerge as a major power. After the Second Punic War, Rome found allies in Rhodes and Athens, and began to advance. After their victory in 146BC they annexed Macedonia and the remaining Greek territories, which became a province of the Roman empire – the eastern half of which formed the basis of the Byzantine Empire, which lasted until 1453AD.

THE OTTOMAN YEARS

Sultan Mehmet II conquered the Byzantine capital Constantinople in 1453, and by 1460 most of Greece was under direct Ottoman rule. The Ottoman system depended heavily on religious communities, and the Greek Orthodox patriarch became extremely powerful. When Ottoman power declined in the 17th and 18th centuries, nationalist movements began to emerge.

The Greek independence war, nurtured by the Friendly Society (Filikí Etería), began in 1821 and ended in 1827 when combined English, French and Russian navies destroyed the Ottoman fleet in the Bay of Navaríno.

MODERN GREECE

The new state was formalised by treaty sessions of 1830, in London. Ioannis Kapodistrias, the first president, was assassinated in 1831. In 1833 the 'Great Powers', England, France and Russia, chose Bavarian Prince Otho as king of Greece.

The *Megáli Idéa* (Great Notion) of redeeming all Greeks living under Ottoman rule, and reconstituting a large part of the Byzantine Empire, was the defining ideology of the new nation, often pursued at the cost of bankrupting

Greece; nonetheless, she did expand incrementally, to reach today's boundaries. The disastrous 1919–23 military expedition into Turkey resulted in humiliating defeat and a huge exchange of populations between the two countries.

After a period of dictatorial rule by the quasi-fascist General Metaxas in the late 1930s, Greece entered World War II. During and after the war, an internal struggle took place between the royalist right and a largely communist left. After the German army withdrew in October 1944, partisan unrest exploded into civil war (1946–49). With American aid, the royalist government crushed the insurrection and instituted tight control over left-wing political activity. The mid-1960s saw a resurgence of centrist and leftist power in George Papandreou's Centre Union government; the royalists connived in its downfall, preparing the ground for the colonels' junta (1967–74), whose human-rights abuses made Greece a pariah. Since the establishment of 'normal' governments and honest elections, the social polarisation of the mid-20th century has subsided, and there is very little to distinguish the platforms of PASOK and Néa Dimokratía. The main issues are now external ones: continuing to improve relations with Turkey, fostering a durable solution to the Cyprus problem, and participating in the workings of the European Union.

Below: naïve painting of a lýra player, Variá, Lésvos
Bottom: café life, Thessaloníki

HISTORICAL HIGHLIGHTS

3000BC Bronze Age Crete: The emergence of the Minoan peoples.

2100–1400BC The great palaces are built by the Minoans.

1400BC The Myceneans built fortified citadels on the Peloponnese.

1200BC Influx of Dorian peoples.

776BC First Olympic games held, the earliest recorded date in Greek history.

8th century–7th century BC The Archaic Period: Emergence of the city-states.

6th century BC Greek city-states control large parts of Mediterranean coast.

550BC Sparta forms the Peloponnesian League with neighbouring city-states.

6th–4th centuries BC The Classical Period. Athens witnesses a great flowering of philosophy and the arts.

490BC Persian leader Darius invades Greece and is defeated at Marathon.

480BC Xerxes invades Greece; overwhelms alliance of city-states at Thermopylae, but is defeated at Salamis.

479BC Persians defeated at Plataea.

454BC The treasury is transferred to Athens, provoking Spartan jealousy.

431–404BC Peloponnesian Wars.

404BC Athens falls and Sparta emerges pre-eminent from the conflict.

382BC Spartan raid on Thebes is repulsed, marking decline of Sparta's power and the resurgence of Athens.

338BC Athens and Thebes are defeated at Chaeronea. All Greece, apart from Sparta, falls under Macedonian rule.

336BC Alexander the Great extends the empire over a vast area.

323BC Alexander dies in Babylon.

322–266BC Failed attempts by Athens and Sparta for independence.

146BC Romans conquer Macedonia and other Greek states. Greece becomes province of Roman empire.

395AD Roman empire divided into eastern and western districts. Greek-dominated Byzantine Empire founded with Constantinople as capital.

1204 Constantinople plundered by Crusaders, assisted by the Venetians.

1453 Constantinople taken by Turks; becomes capital of Ottoman empire.

1460 All Greece, except Crete and east Aegean islands, comes under Ottoman rule. Administration of Greeks entrusted to Orthodox church.

17–18th centuries After growing prosperity, decline in Ottoman power spurs formation of Balkan nationalist movements, notably the *Filikí Etairía* (Friendly Society).

1821 Simultaneous uprisings in various parts of the mainland start Greek War of Independence.

1827 English, French and Russian fleets destroy Ottoman navy at the battle of Navarino.

1830–32 Greece's boundaries set at

London conferences, to include Peloponnese, southern mainland, Sporades and Cyclades islands.

1831 First president, Ioannis Kapodistrias, is assassinated by Maniots.

1833 The 'Great Powers' impose the Bavarian prince Otho as king.

1843–4 Uprising forces Otho to establish constitutional rule and parliamentary government.

1864 Britain cedes Ionian islands to Greece.

1881 Thessaly and southern Epirus granted to Greece by Congress of Berlin.

1897 Greece attacks Turkey in attempt to unite Crete with mainland; failure and near-bankruptcy of the state, but Crete becomes semi-autonomous.

1912–13 The Balkan Wars: Greece takes control of Macedonia, Epirus, Crete and the eastern Aegean.

1919 Venizelos sends troops to Smyrna as prelude to annexing western Anatolia to a "Greater Greece".

1921–3 Greek forces almost reach Ankara but are defeated by Turks under Mustafa Kemal. 390,000 Muslims move to Turkey and 1.3 million Orthodox Christians move to Greece.

1936 George II dissolves parliament; Ioannis Mataxas becomes dictator.

1940 Greek forces push back Italian forces after Mataxas spurns Mussolini's ultimatum.

1941–42 Greece occupied by German, Italian and Bulgarian forces.

Organised resistance, largely communist, begins in mountains.

1944 Greece is liberated by British and communist resistance forces.

1944–49 Imposition of royalist government leads to bitter civil war.

1949–64 Period of right-wing rule under American tutelage; leftists contest elections.

1964–65 George Papandreou's Centre Union briefly governs.

1967–74 Papadopoulos and other colonels stage coup and rule as a military junta.

1974–75 In trying to forcibly annexe Cyprus, the junta falls, Karamanlis returns from exile; republic declared. Free elections, in which Karamanlis' Néa Dimokratía are victors.

1981–89 Greece enters EEC. PASOK wins two elections, with Andreas Papandreou as prime minister.

1990–93 Mitsotakis becomes prime minister, heading *Néa Dimokratía*.

1991 Yugoslav province of Macedonia proclaims independence, provoking bitter dispute with Greece.

1993 PASOK regains power.

1996 Papandreou dies; succeeded by Simitis, who wins early elections.

2000 Simitis narrowly re-elected.

2004 Kostas Karamanlis and Néa Dimokratía defeat PASOK, now led by George Papandreou the younger. Greece successfully hosts the summer Olympic Games.

Map on pages 24–5

1: Athens

Athens (Athína; pop. over 4 million, including Piraeus) is a fascinating place, but conventionally attractive only in spots. Some observers say the ramshackle, Albanian-Turkish pre-Independence village was doomed to become monstrous the moment the capital of Greece was moved here from Náfplio in 1834; others say that Athens was quite liveable until the late 1950s, when ill-advised government policy encouraged thousands to demolish their old houses and erect faceless apartment blocks. But for many local people it is still merely the largest village in the country, *To Megálo Horió*. State-of-the-art nightlife, extensive pedestrian zones, better public transport and rejuvenation of the few remaining historical districts have, since the 1980s, combined to make the city more enjoyable than before.

Preceeding pages: icons for sale
Below: Caryatids on the Erechtheion
Bottom: Kapnikaréa church, Monastiráki

HISTORY

As far back as 1500BC a fortress stood on the Acropolis, one of the three hills dominating central Athens. Over subsequent centuries a town grew around this bluff. Its citizens created the political forms that have been adopted, and adapted, throughout the Western world. During the 7th century BC an aristocratic clique assumed

power, subjecting the rest of the population to an intolerable tax burden.

In 621BC Draco replaced the city's tyrannical laws with his own 'Draconian' laws – stipulating death for almost every offence. He was succeeded by Solon who introduced a judicial system, which served as a landmark in the history of Athens and democracy. Under Pericles there was a period of prosperity in the city and this Golden Age produced the philosopher Socrates and the dramatist Sophocles. A few years after Pericles' death in 429BC, political decline set in, but Athens retained a leading role in the intellectual world until the decline of Roman rule. Only under Byzantine rule did this ancient tradition begin to wane. Paganism was banned, the school of philosophy was closed in the 4th century and in the 6th century AD the Parthenon was converted into a church. After the Ottoman conquest it became a mosque, and the Turkish commander lived on the acropolis. Athens shrank in importance, becoming almost a village. Even its name was corrupted to Setines. But prosperity began to return in 1834 when King Otho made Athens the capital of the newly independent state. Since then, building work has hardly stopped as the city extends its boundaries as far as the steep marble hills.

THE ANCIENT HEART OF THE CITY

Both the Acropolis and ancient agora (*akrópolis* and *agorá* in modern Greek), along with the Pláka, can be seen in a walk lasting four to five hours. In summer, start early to avoid the fierce midday sun. Wear comfortable shoes, perhaps sandals, the same footwear worn by the ancient Athenians as they traversed this quarter.

THE AGORA

The ★ **Monastiráki** ❶ metro station makes an ideal starting point. The lively square in front of the station is named after a small, originally Byzantine, church – an incongruously calm spot amid the hustle and bustle of city life. The

Star Attraction
● The Agora

Athens' environment
Athens has become notorious for the *néfos,* or smog, that hangs over the city in the summer. Caused largely by emissions from vehicles, the pollutants are eating away at the marble monuments for which Athens is so famous. The government has taken some action – cars with even-numbered licence plates are only allowed in on even-numbered days, and vice-versa for odd-numbered vehicles (a rule that is circumvented by many families owning two cars) – but the problem remains. It is exacerbated by the double rush-hour caused by the afternoon siesta. The best hope lies in the new metro system *(see map on page 118)*, which has already taken some traffic off the roads.

The modern Mégaro Mousikís concert hall

Map
below

★★ Classical Agora ② (Apr–Sept: daily
8am–7pm; Oct–Mar: 8am–3pm) is situated
nearby. Some 2,500 years ago, fruit and fish
traders sold their wares here while political ora-
tors honed their skills. In the morning sunshine,
when there are few people about, it is just possible to imagine the atmosphere, sights and smells
on a busy market day. In the 2nd-century BC Stoa
of Attalos colonnade, artisans and scribes would
be hard at work in their studios and offices. The
stoa was rebuilt to house the many finds from

the Agora site , and is a cool place to linger among the scents of ancient herbs replanted by the meticulous American excavators.

On a hill in the northwestern corner of this extensive site stands the **Theseion**, a Classical temple dedicated to Hephaestos, god of metalworkers, and not, as was long believed, to the hero Theseus. With its Doric columns reaching up to the sky, the temple has remained essentially unaltered since 450BC and ranks as one of the best preserved – if rather clunky – examples in Greece.

The Roman Agora

The Roman Agora ❸ stands a few yards from the Classical Agora, behind the tall columns of an old gateway. The striking octagonal Tower of the Winds ❹ dates from the 1st century BC. The tower, which once housed a waterclock, is named after the angelic winged figures on its eight faces, each personifing a wind direction. For a while it was used by Ottoman Dervishes, later as a Catholic church.

ROUTE 1
ATHENS
0 — 300 m

The monument of Lysikratos

Map on pages 24–5

Beyond the Theseion and across Ermoú lies the **Keramikós Cemetery**, the burial ground of ancient Athens, linked to the Agora by a Sacred Way, once lined by bronze statues. The Street of the Tombs, which runs off the Sacred Way, has been excavated and the monuments to wealthy Athenians can be seen along its length.

THE ACROPOLIS

The ★★★ **Acropolis** ❺ (Apr–Sept: daily 8am–7pm; Oct–Mar, daily 8am–4.30pm) towers above the Agora on a limestone bluff . Its history mirrors that of the city. The summit was said to have been the scene of a competition between Athena, goddess of wisdom, and the sea-god Poseidon, for the honour of being the city's patron. Poseidon created a saltwater spring on the Acropolis, but Athena gave the world its first olive tree and the citizens chose her. An olive tree was planted near the Erechtheion to represent her gift.

However, Athena was not infallible in protecting her city; in 480BC the Persians captured Athens and destroyed all the buildings on the Acropolis. Recovery began only in 444BC, when Pericles was leader of Athens and the construction of the new Parthenon began. Work on the impressive entrance, the Propylaia, began in 437BC, just after the Parthenon was finished, and

Below: Temple of Athena Nike
Bottom: the Acropolis

work on the graceful little ★ **Temple of Athena Nike**, now reconstructed, started in 427BC. This, or possibly Sounion, is the spot from which King Aegeus of Athens (after whom the Aegean Sea is named) is believed to have jumped to his death, in the mistaken belief that his son, Theseus, had been killed by the Minotaur on Crete.

THE PARTHENON

The ★★★ **Parthenon**, an indisputed architectural masterpiece, was built between 447 and 438BC under the direction of Iktinos. The designers realised that straight columns would appear thinner in the middle when seen against the brilliant Attic sky, and decided to compensate for this with a technique known as *éntasis*. The columns, and the platform on which they stood, are slightly convex, but owing to a clever optical illusion appear straight. The temple survived more or less intact until 1687, when it suffered a direct hit from Venetian artillery. The Turks were using it as a powder magazine, and the subsequent explosion severely damaged the building. In 1811 most of the friezes were removed by Lord Elgin and transported to the British Museum *(see box)*. In spite of, or perhaps because of, all attempts to destroy it, the majesty of the Parthenon has not been lost.

Marbles controversy
Ever since the Parthenon frieze was 'acquired' by Lord Elgin in the early 19th century there have been calls for the 'Marbles' to be returned to Greece. Fierce lobbying by the Greek government, in particular the late Melina Merkouri, has been met with intransigence by the British authorities, and recent revelations about dubious conservation practices has fired the debate. In the meantime, a new museum is — slowly — being built on the site of the old Makrigianni Barracks just below the Acropolis, that is designed to house *all* the Parthenon sculptures in controlled conditions.

ERECHTHEION

The ★ **Erechtheion**, a temple to Athena and Poseidon, dates from between 421 and 406BC. It was built on the site of more ancient sanctuaries, before which it was the location of a Mycenean palace. In ancient times the restored complex visible today was said to house the original olive tree bequeathed by Athena and the saltwater spring of Poseidon. One wing of the temple, the Porch of the Caryatids, is known for its columns carved in the form of young female captives from ancient Karyai. Today, they are copies, as acid rain was corroding the stone. Four of the originals can be seen in the ★★ **Acropolis Museum**, situated behind the Parthenon (entrance with

Odeon of Herodes Atticus

Map
on pages
24–5

The National Gardens

South of Sýndagma and the Parliament Building are the National Gardens (open sunrise to sunset), full of romantic bowers and arbours, with leafy walks and hidden ponds. The gardens were laid out in the 1840s by Queen Amalia (wife of Otho), who stocked them with plants brought from all over the world. A welcome retreat from the busy streets of central Athens, the gardens are a pleasant place to while away the time.

Temple of the Olympian Zeus

Acropolis ticket); Elgin sold another to the British Museum, while the sixth is unaccounted for.

THEATRES

The view from the Acropolis, to the south, includes two theatres directly beneath the rock. The vast ★★ **Odeon of Herodes Atticus ❻** is used during the summer for the Athens Festival. Built by the Romans in the 2nd century AD, it can accommodate several thousand spectators (tickets and programme information from the theatre box office: www.hellenicfestival.gr; tel 210 32 21 459). The ★★ **Theatre of Dionysos ❼** is said to be Europe's oldest. Surviving marble seating tiers date from around 320BC and later, but scholars are agreed that many dramas by such celebrated playwrights as Aeschylus, Sophocles, Euripides and Aristophanes were first staged here at religious festivals in the 5th century BC. A state subsidy for theatre-goers meant that every Athenian citizen could take time off to attend.

Continuing down Dionysíou Areopagítou to where it joins Amalías brings you to **Hadrian's Arch**, built by that Roman emperor to delineate the Greek from the Roman city. Also nearby is the ★ **Temple of the Olympian Zeus** (daily Apr–Sept: 8am–7pm; Oct–Mar: daily 8am–3pm). This was the largest temple in Greece and, while completed by Hadrian, initially dates from around 600BC.

PLAKA

Pedestrianised Dionysíou Areopagítou leads past the entrances to both theatres. The route back to the old town, **Pláka ❽**, beginning from the bottom of this street, passes the **Monument of Lysikratos ❾**. This strange cylindrical structure once housed a bronze tripod which Lysikratos, a wealthy Athenian, won as a prize in the Dionysian Festival, in about 335BC. During the 17th and 18th centuries, the monument was part of a Capuchin convent, and Lord Byron supposedly stayed in it.

ADRIANOU STREET

Pláka's longest street, lined with souvenir shops and crowded with tourists from around the world, leads back down to Monastiráki square and metro station. Just before you arrive, you'll notice **Hadrian's Library**, a vast site still being excavated, and the **Tzisdarákis Mosque** (Apr–Sept: Tues–Sun 8am–7pm; Oct–Mar: Tues–Sun 8.30am–3pm), home to a small display of Greek folk ceramics – although the building's interior is equally interesting.

Star Attractions
● Theatre of Dionysus
● Lykavittós

Below: evzone on guard in Sýndagma
Bottom: Lykavittós by night

THE MAIN SQUARES

The two main squares, **Constitution** (Platía Syndágmatos) ⓫ and **Omónia** (Platía Omónias) ⓬ are busy places, the more so since they became main transfer stations on Athens' metro system. Banks, travel agencies, hotels and a post office border Sýntagma on three sides, while the Neoclassical **Parliament Building** (Voulí) ⓭, formerly the royal palace, stands to the east. It is guarded by soldiers *(evzone)* dressed in traditional white pleated kilts, the *foustanélla*, and *tsaroúhia* (pom-pom shoes). Omónia is choked with traffic by day; six boulevards meet here and a large metro station lurks underneath. Cafés and *períptera* (kiosks) line the pavements, jostling for space with lottery sellers and itinerant vendors.

Map on pages 24–5

KOLONAKI

★ **Kolonáki** ⓮ – a well-maintained square in an upmarket quarter of Athens – is a more elegant spot. The cafés are more exclusive, and nearby clothes shops specialise in expensive fashions. ★★ **Lykavittós** ⓯ rises northeast of Kolonáki. A white chapel dedicated to Ágios Geórgios stands on top of the hill, and particularly at night, the summit offers an unbeatable view over the city.

Museums

Below: the mask of 'Agamemnon'
Bottom: the Neoclassical National Library on Panepistimíou

Now reopened after a protracted renovation, the ★★★ **National Archaeological Museum** ⓰ (Mon 12.30–5pm, Tues–Fri 8am–5pm, Sat–Sun 8.30am–3pm) should not be missed, for its its exhibits trace the various artistic styles of Greek antiquity, from early Cycladic to Roman. The refurbishment to some extent scrambled the old gallery order, so be sure to lay hands on an up-to-date catalogue to locate the most interesting works. Regardless of the result of the reshuffle, certain works have retained pride of place, for example the best of the free-standing bronze statues, a 5th-century BC Poseidon with outstretched arm, in the act of hurling a now-vanished trident. The Mycenaean Collection has been kept together, with its focus the death mask which Heinrich Schliemann found in Mycenae and took

to be that of King Agamemnon, although it is actually a couple of centuries too early. The superb frescoes from Akrotíri on Santoríni portray delicate antelopes, blue monkeys and swallows flying above lilies.

The other major museums are back in the centre. One of the best is the ★★ **Benáki Museum** in Kolonáki (Koumbári 1; Mon, Wed, Fri–Sat 9am–5pm, Thur 9am–midnight, Sun 9am–3pm). Its collection includes Byzantine and post-Byzantine icons, folk costumes, ancient jewellery, historical documents and assorted engravings and paintings. Nearby is the highly recommended ★★ **Goulandrís Museum of Cycladic and Ancient Greek Art** (Neofýtou Douká; Mon, Wed–Fri 10am–4pm, Sat 10am–3pm). Based on a private collection, the beautifully displayed exhibits chart the changing artefacts of the Bronze Age Aegean peoples. The museum also houses one of the largest and most important collections of later ancient Greek pottery. The **Byzantine and Christian Museum** (Kolonáki, Vassilísis Sofías 22; Tues–Sun 8.30am–3pm) is also worth a visit. Set in an 1848 villa, it has an extensive collection of Byzantine and post-Byzantine icons.

In Pláka are the excellent **Museum of Greek Popular Musical Instruments** (Diogénous 1–3; Tues, Thur–Sun 10am–2pm, Wed noon–6pm), with music samples and a CD shop, plus the **Museum of Greek Folk Art** (Kydathinéon 17; Tues–Sun 10am–2pm), its highlight a series of murals by the folk artist Theophilos.

EXCURSIONS

Piraeus (Pireás) merges seamlessly with Athens, and the metro line ends directly alongside the harbour. Huge ferries, variable-sized catamarans and small hydrofoils moor at various points of the quay. Boards outside ticket offices give details of sailings to the various islands, and everywhere there is the frenzied atmosphere of imminent departure. There's nothing in particular to see except for the excellent **archaeological museum** (Hariláou Trikoúpi 31; Tues–Sun 8.30am–3pm),

Star Attractions
● National Museum
● Benaki Museum
● Goulandrís Museum

Exárhia, Pangráti, Méts
These three districts, each with its own identity, lie on the edge of central Athens. Exárhia lies around the National Museum and was famed as the centre of radical student politics. It has since lost that distinction but now has some of the best nightlife in the city. Méts, south of the National Gardens, is home to the huge Próto Nekrotafío (First Cemetery) where the great and good of Athens are buried. Finally, Pangráti, east and north of the Olympic Stadium, is a quiet residential quarter that has some excellent local tavernas.

Leaving from Piraeus

Map on pages 34–5

Map on pages 34–5

Salamína

This, the closest of the Argo-Saronic islands to Athens, is half-an-hour away from Piraeus by boat, and many people commute between the island and the city. It was famed in antiquity as the location of the naval battle of Salamis where, in 480BC, the Greeks defeated the Persian fleet – part of the invasion force of Xerxes. Perhaps the greatest site of interest to visitors on the island is the late 17th-century Faneroméni Monastery.

with an Archaic bronze *kouros* dedicated to Apollo. ★**Kessariani** (Tues–Sun 8am–2.30pm) is an 11th-century monastery occupying a pretty site on the green slopes of Mount Hymettus (Ymittós) overlooking the town.

SOUNION

Situated at the windy tip of the Attic peninsula, ★★**Cape Soúnion**, some 70km (45 miles) from Athens, is a romantic spot, although it is impossible to be alone. The sun sinks behind the columns of the **Temple of Poseidon** (Tues–Sun 10am–sunset), which stands at the top of a steep cliff. Completed in 440BC, its slender, salt-white columns are still a landmark for ships. Lord Byron carved his name in a column on the north side. In the bay below are the remains of ancient ship sheds. Get a bus from Mavromatéon by the Pédion Áreos, or on Filellínon, near Sýndagma.

AEGINA

Aegina: Temple of Aphaea

Sleepy ★★★**Aegina** (Égina) is a welcome relief from the hectic atmosphere of Athens. The strategically placed island became a leading maritime power after the 7th century BC. It sided with Athens at the Battle of Salamis in 480BC, but was continuously at odds with its neighbour; the Athenians deported the population at the beginning of the Peloponnesian War, and the island never really recovered, although it did regain some prosperity in the 15th century. Under Ottoman rule it became a modestly successful commercial centre, specialising in the cultivation of pistachio nuts. One of Greece's best known temples is here: the 5th-century BC **Temple of Aphaea** (Mon–Fri 8am–7pm), a local deity related to Artemis, on a wooded crest at the island's northeastern tip.

HYDRA AND POROS

With its romantic harbour town ★★**Hydra** (Ídra) is worth at least a one-day visit. Once no more than a small port, increased commerce during the

17th and 18th centuries enabled Hydra to emerge as one of the dominant islands in the Aegean. Tthe resulting wealth paid for the imposing mansions of merchant families. The narrow alleys and steep staircases, plus a ban on cars, give Hydra a special charm. ★ **Póros** is also well worth a visit. Built on a hill, the pastel-shaded town resembles an inverted amphitheatre and is quite stunning.

Star Attractions
- Souníon
- Aegina
- Hydra

Below: Hydra
Bottom: Soúnion

SPÉTSES

★ **Spétses**, the remotest of the Argo-Saronic islands, still has a covering of woodland and more sandy beaches than its neighbours. Spétses' wealth came from shipping and the tradition of shipbuilding is still maintained. Like Hydra, Póros and Aegina, it can be reached by hydrofoil or slow ferry from Aktí Tselépi in Piraeus.

ÉVVIA

★ **Évvia** (Euboea) is the second-biggest island, after Crete. Athenians seek tranquillity in the hilly north of the island, with its forests and broad beaches; at the old port of **Límni** in the northwest; or at the seafood tavernas south of the main town, Halkída. If you've a car, use one of four ferry services crossing at various points; otehwise take a fast train to Halkídha, then continue by bus.

The Moreás

The Peloponnese (Pelopónnisos in Greek) takes its name from the legendary hero Pelops, plus the Greek word for island, *nísos*. Joined only to the mainland by a tiny isthmus, cut across by the Corinth Canal, the peninsula is almost is an island. The medieval name, the Moreás, is now seldom used. It derives from the word for mulberry *(mouriá)* because the peninsula is shaped like a mulberry leaf.

A friendly smile from Hydra

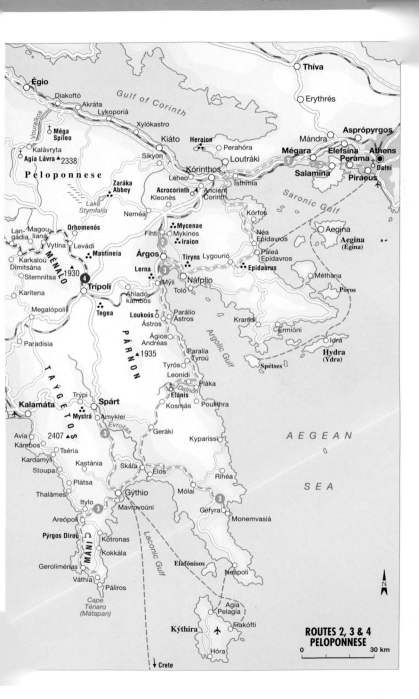

ROUTES 2, 3 & 4
PELOPONNESE

0   30 km

Map
on pages
34–5

2: The Argolid Peloponnese

Athens – Ancient Corinth – Epidaurus – Náfplio – Mycenae (210km/130 miles)

The history of mainland Greece begins in the Argolid peninsula at the northeast corner of the Peloponnese. The apostle Paul preached to the Corinthians, and in Epidaurus, the world's first spa town, the semi-mythical Asklepios laid the foundations for modern medicine. King Otho not only moved the country's capital from Náfplio to Athens in 1834, he also brought beer from Bavaria – brewed by one Klaus Fuchs, his name corrupted to the still-extant brand 'Fix'. Finally, behind the Lion Gate at Mycenae, lies the palace of Agamemnon. Allow a minimum of four days for the cited attractions, although a week would be more comfortable. For those dependent on the bus, Náfplio makes the best base.

Below: Dafní monastery mosaic
Bottom: Ancient Corinth

DAFNI AND LOUTRAKI

On the way from Athens to the Peloponnese, **Dafní Monastery**, at the very western edge of the city, is a good place to break the journey. The 11th-century mosaics in the Byzantine church have just emerged from a lengthy restoration; the high point in all senses is the Christ Pandokrator (Ruler of All) in the dome, the best surviv-

ing example of such an image in Greece, but the cycle of images – including scenes from the life of Christ and the Virgin – is unusually complete.

Loutráki, some 80km (50 miles) from Athens, is probably the best-known spa in the country, lending its name to the best-selling brand of mineral water. In recent years a restored train service from Athens has supplemented buses, and the opening of a casino has further boosted the place's appeal to a wider audience. The pebble beach is negligible, but allegedly therapeutic water gushes from the springs in the baths, which are decorated with some superb mosaics. Tavernas and restaurants line the promenade; one sea-view café has a three-stage waterfall flowing past its tables.

THE CORINTH CANAL

The road to modern Kórinthos (90km/55 miles from Athens) crosses the ★**isthmus** where the famous Corinth Canal separates the Peloponnese from the mainland. From the 70-m (230-ft) high bridge it is possible to peer down directly into the water below. The Roman emperor Nero had plans to cut a watercourse through the rock, but it wasn't until 1893 that the channel was completed. Even before the era of supertankers, the canal quickly became obsolete, but the isthmus is now a tourist attraction and tour coaches and service buses break their journeys here. Souvenir shops and fast-food restaurants teeter close to the edge of the gaping canal cutting.

ANCIENT CORINTH

The modern town of Kórinthos, beyond the canal, has few attractions to prompt a visit; its transport connections are of most interest. There are trains to Athens, Pátra, Árgos and Trípoli, but bus stations and stops are scattered confusingly across the town – the most important are opposite the railway station, on Aratoú, and on Koliátsou.

The ruins of ★★★ **Ancient Corinth** (Arhéa ´órinthos; museum and excavated site: summer: ily 8.30am–7pm; winter: 8am–5pm), domi-

Star Attraction
● Ancient Corinth

> **Ancient sanctuaries**
> Beyond Loutráki lies the **Perahora Heraion** at Cape Melangávi, with an Archaic Hera temple and a stoa. Another important ancient sanctuary, venue for the quadrennial Isthmian games, can be found at **Isthmia** on the southwest side of the canal; the Roman baths here retain extensive floor mosaics of sea creatures, real and imaginary.

Acrocorinth, fortifications

Map
on pages
34–5

👁 **Temple of Apollo**
Of the few remaining upright pillars, the seven from the Greek Temple of Apollo date from the 6th century BC. These Doric pillars were carved from solid stone and not, as was usual, assembled from a number of drums. Finds from Greek and Roman times, such as Corinthian vases and capitals adorned with acanthus leaves, can be seen in the museum. Ask at the entrance for a plan of the excavations. Despite its ruined state, the Temple of Apollo still looks impressive.

Acrocorinth

nated by the huge acropolis of Acrocorinth, are well worth negotiating the modern town to find. The ancient town was established in the 8th century BC and became a prosperous centre, thanks to its geographical position and the availability of two harbours: Lechaion on the Gulf of Corinth and Kenchreai on the Saronic Gulf. Corinth founded colonies in the Mediterranean basin, one of which was the important port of Syracuse. Trade in Corinthian pottery flourished, but the Romans destroyed the lively city in 146BC.

ROMAN CORINTH

Few buildings of Greek origin remain, as Julius Caesar oversaw the reconstruction of the town in 44BC. The ruins of the Roman **agora** occupy much of the excavated site. The outline of colonnades and the vaulting for rows of shops are discernible. The odeon, theatre and law courts were all destroyed by an earthquake and by invading Goths in the 4th century AD. The pavement on the **Lechaion Road** and the remains of the **Fountain of Peirene** have been well preserved. Only the plinth remains from the podium on which St Paul preached in AD54. The goddess of love, Aphrodite, was worshipped up in Acrocorinth. In its heyday, temple prostitution was rife, and St Paul was presented with a considerable challenge as he attempted to change people's ways.

ACROCORINTH

On the crest of the steep grey rock, looming above the excavations, stands the ★★**Acrocorinth** fortress. The function of the acropolis at Ancient Corinth changed over the centuries. The towers and battlements of Acrocorinth have been adapted by the Byzantines, the Latin Crusaders, the Venetians and the Ottomans. There is no bus to the summit and those not willing to make the 4-km (2-mile) trek will have to take a taxi or come in a hired car. Sturdy footwear is advisable when visiting the fortress. Entry is via three successiv gates, respectively Turkish, Venetian-Frankis and Byzantine. The heart of the fortifications is mainly Byzantine, but some sections date from the 4th century BC. In the spring, poppies and yellow daisies flower between the walls. There is a tremendous view from the summit encompassing the surrounding hilly countryside and the Gulf of Corinth. By late afternoon, the site will be empty and only a tinkling bell will occasionally interrupt the silence – shepherds often graze their sheep between the remains of the Aphrodite temple and the 2-km (1-mile) circuit of walls.

Star Attractions
- **Acrocorinth**
- **Epidaurus**

ON FROM CORINTH

The Saronic Gulf slowly comes into view as the road continues on to Epidaurus. On a clear day some of the offshore islands will be visible. About 140km (90 miles) from Athens, set in a lemon grove, lies the pretty Classical amphitheatre at ★ **Paleá Epídavros** just past Néa Epídavros; more ruins are being uncovered by ongoing excavations. Buses link Paleá Epídavros and Epidaurus with Athens, Corinth and Náfplio.

Below: oranges
Bottom: Epidaurus

EPIDAURUS

Most tourists head straight for ★★★ **Epidaurus** (Epídavros in modern Greek; 155km/95 miles from Athens; museum and theatre: daily,

Map
on pages
34–5

Below: Náfplio café
Bottom: Boúrtzi island

8am–7pm), where they will find an almost completely preserved theatre dating from the 4th century BC. The auditorium, with seating for 12,000 people, forms a part of the wooded hillside, and the mountains opposite provide a natural backdrop. The theatre's acoustics are remarkable: even from the highest of the 54 rows, it is possible to hear a coin fall on the marble floor of the circular orchestra pit. Live theatre (classical Greek drama) comes to the ancient site from June to August, as part of the Hellenic Festival (tickets from festival box office in Athens, www.hellenicfestival.gr for current address; or on the day at the theatre or from travel agents in Náfplio).

In antiquity many of the visitors were invalids, as the remains of the 4th-century BC **Sanctuary of Asklepios** lie near the theatre. Asklepios, the son of Apollo, was revered as the god of healing. The concentric walls of the *tholos* (beehive) have puzzled historians. Was it a place where the priests underwent ritual initiation, or did it house snakes, which were required for some treatments? The adjoining building, the *abaton*, was a colonnade that served as a dormitory for patients. Dreams were recounted to priests, who analysed them to help make a diagnosis. Theatre was said to divert the attention of patients away from their complaint – an ancient form of psychotherapy. The Shrine of Asklepios was later

used by doctors who dispensed medicines and carried out operations. They placed great value on the healing powers of nature and were aware of the importance of a healthy diet.

The museum contains statues of Asklepios, also known as Aesculapius, often shown holding a staff with a snake coiled around it. The staff is now used as a symbol of medical science.

NAFPLIO

★★**Náfplio** (180km/110 miles) is a delightful town. In 1830 it became the capital of newly independent Greece; now it's merely the administrative centre of the province of Argolída. King Otho lived here briefly before moving his capital to Athens in 1834; since then the old quarter has undergone a long and gentle decline. Outside of Kérkyra Town on Corfu it is the the best preserved Venetian town in Greece, for it was one of Venice's main strongholds on the Peloponnese.

AROUND TOWN

Shuttered Venetian facades and Ottoman mosques characterise the old town. The larger mosque on **Platía Syndágmatos** was used as the meeting place for Greece's first parliament; another nearby began life as a Catholic church, while a third served briefly as a cinema. The Venetian barracks now house an archaeological museum (Tues–Sun 8.30am–3pm), where the highlight is a Mycenaean bronze suit of armour . The marble-paved *platía* is ringed by cafés. The old town is built against the north slope of a steep bluff, with streets higher up or close to the waterfront cooled a bit by breezes off the Argolid Gulf. If you want a proper swim head to the beach of **Karathóna**, extending south from the other side of the bluff. Opposite the quay lies the island-fortress of the **Boúrtzi**. In the 15th century, the Venetians chose its site at the entrance to the harbour, which enabled them to close off the port with a chain in time of war. The angular tower, which gives the island the appearance of a ship, came later.

Star Attraction
• Náfplio

Assassination
Náfplio is (in)famous as the place where Greece's first prime minister, Ioannis Kapodistrias, was murdered. At independence he faced the difficult task of uniting the disparate factions that had fought against the Turks. Some of these suspected Kapodistrias of concentrating power in his own hands and, in 1831, he was shot by two leaders from the Máni. This did not, in the end, further their aims, as the so-called 'Great Powers' then imposed the autocratic King Otho on Greece, who ruled through his Bavarian advisors.

Náfplio street scene

Map on pages 34–5

Palamídi

FORTRESSES

Both fortresses above the town are of Venetian origin, and protected the harbour from the 14th to 16th centuries. **Akronáfplia**, built on Byzantine walls and often known by its later Turkish name Íts Kalé, overlooks the tiled roofs of the old town, but sadly the fortress has been sullied by the 1960s-era Xenia Palace luxury hotel. The **★★Palamídi** is a more easterly complex of fortresses that dominate the town. If you make the 1,000-step ascent to the top you will be rewarded with a tremendous view over Náfplio, the sea and the mountains of Argolída. At the beginning of the 18th century the Venetians ringed the original fortifications with a huge wall that extended far over the mountain ridge. The fortress may also be reached by car from the village of Prónia.

There are bus connections from Nápflio to Kórinthos and Athens, Spárti, Paleá Epídavros, Epidaurus, Mycenae and Toló; there is no longer a hydrofoil service, but a revived train service via Árgos calls at a new station near the edge of town.

TOLO AND ÁRGOS

Just 10km (6 miles) south of Náfplio lies the beach resort of Toló. Modern **Árgos**, a few kilometres northwest, occupies the site of ancient Argos; this busy commercial town can offer an archaeological museum superior to Náfplio's, plus at the outskirts one of the most steeply raked ancient theatres in Greece.

Hotel Belle Hèlène

By far the nicest and most atmospheric place to stay in Mykínes is the Hotel Belle Helène. Previously this was the house where Heinrich Schliemann stayed while he was excavating at Mycenae and it has been preserved largely as it was then. The visitors' book has an illustrious list of names, including Virginia Woolf and Claude Debussy.

MYCENAE

One of the oldest sites in Greek history is found near Náfplio at **★★★Mycenae** (210km/130 miles from Athens). The wall-masonry here is so massive it was thought that Perseus, the son of Zeus, had to call on the Cyclops to help him lift the stones – thus the term 'Cyclopean', erroneously applied to almost any thick, ancient wall. The Mycenaeans (sometimes called the Achaeans) lived in the fortress (summer: daily 8am–7pm; winter 8.30am–5pm) near the modern village o

Mykínes. Mycenae was the leading power on the Peloponnese from 1600–1150BC. The Myceneans had links with Crete, and the Minoans had some influence on the life and culture of the mainland.

Heinrich Schliemann, a German archaeologist and businessman, captivated by the Homeric story of the Mycenaean heroes in the Trojan war, of King Agamemnon and his army, set out to find the original home of the Mycenaeans. Using only the descriptions given by Homer, he achieved what many thought impossible, discovering in 1876 what he believed to be the family tomb of Agamemnon. It transpired that he had actually found the grave of a king who lived two centuries before the Homeric wars, but he had unearthed one of the most fascinating sites in Greece.

HISTORY AND MYTH

The yellowy-brown walls, built with huge stone blocks, rise out of a bare, sun-baked hill. Behind them, c.1350BC (the approximate date of the semi-legendary Trojan War), lived Mycenaean kings, craftsmen and artists. The site is now quiet and peaceful and yet, according to the legend, it was the scene of terrible deeds. It was in Mycenae that, at the behest of his wife Clytemnestra, Agamemnon was murdered, partly in revenge for the sacrifice of their daughter Iphigenia at Aulis.

Star Attraction
● **Mycenae**

Below: Peloponnesian vine
Bottom: Mycenae

Map on pages 34–5

To avenge the death of his father, Orestes, spurred on by his sister Electra, then killed their mother. Thus was fulfilled the curse against Atreus, the father of Agamemnon. Atreus had his brother's children killed, and then served them to their father for supper. He responded to this outrage with the curse, which devastated the next two generations of the so-called Atreid dynasty.

THE SITE

Below: the Lion Gate
Bottom: the Treasury of Atreus

As the afternoon sun baths the hill of Mycenae in warm light, it is hard to imagine the dramatic fulfilment of the curse. Instead of warriors and chariots, thousands of tourists pass through the **Lion Gate** each day. One of the oldest stone carvings in Europe, created from one huge stone in about 1250BC, marks the entrance to the fortress. Two headless relief lions stand on a triangular pediment. The threshold stone showing the deep ruts made by chariots entering the town has been removed to prevent further damage. To the right, surrounded by upright gravestones, lie the graves in which Schliemann found 15kg (33lbs) of gold. These treasures are now in the National Archaeological Museum in Athens. The golden mask, an imprint of the face, and the gold decorations on the sword, demonstrate how skilled the Mycenaeans were at shaping this precious metal.

A wide ramp leads from the Lion Gate past the graves to the remains of the Royal Palace. With a little imagination you can make out the reception room and throne room from the foundations. Beneath the hill on the road towards Mykínes stands the **Treasury of Atreus**, actually a large domed tomb. A track known as a *dromos* leads into the interior. In the half-light an enormous dome can just be made out. The Mycenaeans used a sophisticated method of construction to create this: every ring of stone in the roof overlaps the ring below very slightly, so the whole construction is self-supporting.

There are trains from Mykínes station to Kórinthos and Náfplio, and buses to Athens, Náfplio and Árgos.

3: South to Máni

Náfplio – Gýthio/Máni – Mystrás (220km/135 miles).

Map on pages 34–5

Mountains, wild landscapes and fortified villages are the distinguishing features of this journey to the southern tip of the Peloponnese. The road as far as Leonídi is one of the finest stretches of coastal road in Greece, with the steep Párnon mountains on one side and miles of shingle beach on the other. The picturesque port of Gýthio serves as the gateway to the Máni peninsula, one of the most arid and eerie corners of Greece. Here at the 'end of the world' was thought to be the mythical entrance to the underworld. North from Gýthio is Mystrás, the Byzantine ghost town. Allow at least three days for this tour. A bus runs to Leonídi via Árgos and from there you can take a taxi to Gýthio, though it's far better to rent a car in Náfplio.

THE EAST COAST

Between Náfplio *(see page 41)* and Leonídi, the Aegean is never far away, lapping the coast of this little-visited region known as **Kynouría**. Parálio Ástros is the first beach resort here, overlooked by a little castle and the perfect spot for a refreshing dip in the sea. The next relatively lively tourist

Tiryns
This Mycenaean citadel is close to Náfplio. Although less remains of the palace itself than at Mycenae, the 'Cyclopean' walls are impressive – as a naturally less defensive site the walls had to be correspondingly bigger. The site also has a secret stairway leading down to a rear gate, and a corbel-ceilinged gallery whose walls have been rubbed smooth by the generations of sheep that have sheltered there.

The Maniot skyline

Map on pages 34–5

Below: Elónis Monastery
Bottom: the Párnon Mountains

centre en route is **Paralía Tyroú**, popular with Greek holidaymakers because of its pebble beach. The same is true of **Leonídi** (80km/50 miles). Easter festivities in this country town of 7,000 inhabitants draw big crowds who celebrate with spit-roasted lamb and dancing. A number of unusual customs and an old dialect, Tsakonian, have been retained in this region at the foot of rusty-red palisades. Sumptuous, walled estates give an indication of the wealth the townsfolk once enjoyed from their enterprise as sea-captains and traders.

Nowadays, the fertile coastal plain at the mouth of the **Dafnón Gorge** provides a living for local farmers. An avenue flanked by citrus groves, olive trees and aubergine and tomato fields leads to the idyllic port of Pláka, even more tranquil now that the summer hydrofoil service between there and Monemvasiá or Piraeus has ceased – Kyparíssi down the coast is the nearest active port.

The road winds its way inland following the bed of the Dafnón Gorge before beginning to climb in earnest. After you have negotiated some spectacular bends, the **Elónis Monastery** comes into view, clinging to the vertical rock face like a swallow's nest. Near an icon-filled chapel is a spring that is supposed to have medicinal powers. The monastery is now maintained by a small community of nuns.

GYTHIO

Beyond the mountain village of **Kosmás** and the minor Byzantine centre of Geráki *(see page 48)* lies ★ **Gýthio** (165km/100 miles). Brightly painted fishing boats bob in the small harbour, with white-washed and pastel-coloured houses nestling on the slopes – a postcard setting for a meal in a seafood taverna. The offshore island of **Marathonísi**, linked to the mainland by a causeway, is said to be the ancient island of **Kranae**. According to legend, when Paris abducted Helen, they spent their first night together there – and it remains a romantic spot.

From Gýthio there are buses to Areópoli, Pýrgos Diroú, GerolIménas, Monemvasiá, Spárti, Trípoli and Athens; ferries go to Kýthira, western Crete and very occasionally Piraeus.

THE MANI

Gýthio is a good starting point for an excursion into the ★★ **Máni**, the middle of the three peninsulas at the south end of the Peloponnese. Cross the peninsula towards Areópoli, first passing the sandy beach at **Mavrovoúni**, an excellent spot for windsurfing, with camp-sites and tavernas. Suddenly the landscape is dominated by so-called 'tower houses', where feuding Maniot families hid by day, emerging at night to bring in supplies of food and water. Until the 19th century this remote corner was a stormy oligarchy of feuding families who waged vendettas over land, water, honour and women. Fierce enough when fighting each other, their ruthlessness knew no bounds when faced with an outside enemy, whether Goth, Slav or Turk. Some of the ruined houses in **Areópoli** have been restored and turned into guesthouses. The Maniots were as pious as they were fierce, and the countryside is dotted with ancient churches, some of them frescoed and most of them locked to protect their treasures.

It is well worth a detour to see the caves at ★★ **Pýrgos Diroú** (May–Sept: daily 8am–7pm; Oct–Apr: 8am–3pm), although in peak season you may have to wait two hours to get in, as group

Star Attractions
● Máni peninsula
● Váthia

A stormy sky over the Máni

Laments
The Máni is home to a strong tradition of lamenting, known as *mirológia*. These are an important part of the death and mourning ritual – especially so in an area where frequent blood feuds often lead to the death of family members. An exclusively female tradition, it not only assists in the process of saying farewell to the dead, but in expressing and negotiating women's frustrations and anxieties in a male-dominated society.

Map on pages 34–5

Kýthira

Off the southern coast of the Peloponnese lies the island of Kýthira. Although it is considered part of the Ionian islands – it shares a common history of Venetian and British rule – it is governed from Piraeus as part of the Argo-Saronic Islands, and architecturally it exhibits a hybrid of Cycladic and Ionian styles. The island is easily reached by ferry from Gýthio or Neápoli, and is becoming increasingly popular with Greek tourists.

Pýrgos Diroú caves

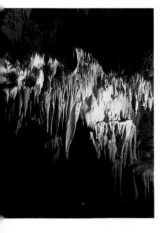

size is limited. An underground lake has been formed by water seeping through the porous limestone. Rowing boats take visitors into an enchanting underworld, where the waters mirror the twists and folds of red and yellow stalactites.

The landscape becomes increasingly barren as the road heads south. Peasants once expended considerable energy constructing terraces to retain the last crumb of soil, but only stunted olive trees grow there now. At the southernmost tip, **Akrotíri Ténaro (Cape Mátapan)**, bare rocks reach up from the sea. Nothing stands between here, the legendary entrance to Hades, and Africa; after Gibraltar it is the most southerly point of the European mainland. The gate of the underworld is a yawning sea-cave on the promontory's east shore.

LAKONIA

The Máni is a sub-district of the region, and province, of Lakonía. Before continuing to modern Spárti, the fortified town of ★★ **Monemvasiá** is worth a detour. This almost impregnable town, draped over a huge crag overlooking the sea, was a strategically important trading post and fortress on the route from Italy to Africa and Constantinople. Some inviting hotels and inns are hidden away in the narrow alleys that wind between the Byzantine churches and Venetian-influenced houses of the lower town. The upper town, on the summit, has lain in ruins for centuries now.

Between Monemvasiá and Spárti is another Byzantine site, the large village of ★ **Geráki**. Less visited than either Monemvasiá or Mystrás, the setting is nonetheless impressive and the scattered churches here are decorated with original frescoes. Geráki passed into the hands of the Crusaders after the Fourth Crusade, and Geráki's largest church, Ágios Geórgios stands within their fortified acropolis. It was built in 1256 by Jean de Nivelet and its design is based on the castle at Mystrás. The other local churches, however, are scattered around the town, and you will need to engage the services of the caretaker to find and unlock them.

MYSTRAS

Head north now to **Spárti** (215km/135 miles).
This truly spartan town would have little to offer
the tourist, other than regular bus services to
Gýthio, Monemvasiá and Athens, were it not for
the Byzantine ruin of ★★★ **Mystrás** (summer:
daily 8am–7pm; winter 8am–2pm). It lies on a
rocky outcrop of Mount Taýgetos, high above the
fertile plain created by the Evrótas River. The
Crusader Villehardouin built a castle here in 1249,
but it was captured by the Byzantines in 1265.
The houses, churches and palaces beneath the
rock became a centre for Byzantine culture,
before being captured by the Ottomans in 1460.
Under a brief Venetian rule in the 18th century the
town recovered, but most inhabitants deserted
Mystrás when King Otho built modern Spárti.

Striking features are the red-tiled roofs of the
renovated churches in the lower town. The frescoes in the **Perívleptos Monastery** are the best
preserved in Mystrás, although they are rivalled
by those in **Odigítria** church, attached to the
Vrondóhion monastery. Painters from Serbia,
Constantinople and Italy worked at Perívleptos –
the influence of the latter is evident in many frescoes. Nuns still live in the **Pandánassa Convent**,
where blind Gothic arches decorate the walls. The
impressive walls of the **Palace of the Despots**
(closed for restoration) dominate the upper town.

Star Attractions
• **Pýrgos Diroú**
• **Monemvasiá**
• **Mystrás**

Below: Monemvasiá
Bottom: frescoed ceiling,
Perívleptos, Mystrás

Map
on pages
34–5

*Below: Arcadian landscape
Bottom: battling with the
Centaurs, Olympia Museum*

4: Arcadia

**Trípoli – Dimitsána – Olympia – Pátra (260km/
160 miles).**

It was some 2,000 years ago that ancient Greek
athletes first met to honour Zeus at Olympia. The
venue for this famous event still has a magical
appeal. The Cretan author Nikos Kazantzakis
wrote that no other place in Greece reminded him
'so sweetly and so constantly of peace', and a day-
trip through the mountains of Arcadia is reward-
ing. The people of this raw mountain region
tending their livestock by the roadside have developed skills as artisans, particularly woodcarvers
and stonemasons. Samples of their work can be
seen in the villages of Vytína and Langádia. Idyllic sandy beaches lie to the west of Olympia, and
the Kyllíni peninsula is where the ancient Greeks
went to recover from their Olympic exertions.

TRIPOLI

Trípoli (pop. 22,000) lies at the heart of a fertile plateau about an hour's travel from Náfplio
or Spárti. The capital of Arcadia is the economic
heart of the region and an important junction,
though since the town was razed during the Greek
war of independence, there is little of interest to
see. The railway, bus services and trunk roads

(including the recently built motorway from Kórinthos) all meet here. There are buses to Olympia and Pátra, Athens via Náfplio, Spárti and thence Kalámata, as well as trains to Athens via Kórinthos and Árgos, and Kalamáta.

THE ARCADIAN MOUNTAINS

The main westbound highway heads out of Trípoli towards Pýrgos and Pátra through the mountains of Arcadia. Beyond Levídi fir forests cover the slopes of the 2,000-m (6,500-ft) **Ménalo** range. The woodcarving village of ★ **Vytína** at an altitude of 1,000m (3,250ft) benefits from the cool mountain air; even in mid-summer the temperature is always bearable. Woodcarving has a long tradition in Vytína, and the church interior, with choir stalls, prayer stools and altars, testifies to the skills of local craftsmen. Souvenirs such as shepherds' crooks and salad serving-sets are on sale in the shops around the church square. The *Aïdonia* taverna serves delicious food, such as home-made pasta with braised beef or lamb, and wine from the barrel.

DIMITSANA AND THE LOUSIOS GORGE

Some 60km (38 miles) from Trípoli, a short distance south of the highway, lies ★ **Dimitsána** (pop. 500). A viewpoint on the access road offers a splendid view over this mountain village. Stone houses with wooden balconies and red-tiled roofs cling to a ridge and then climb over the summit of a hill, while below, a stream surges through the verdant ★ **Loúsios Gorge** and goat bells ring along its banks. Walking routes lead south through the steep-sided canyon to the Byzantine monasteries of **Néa** and **Paleá Filosófou**, and the still-inhabited monastery of **Agíou Ioánnou Prodrómou**, clinging to the left bank of the gorge.

The whole region around Dimitsána and its sister village **Stemnítsa**, above Agiou Ioánnou Prodrómou, was a crucial focal point of resistance to the Ottomans; before the revolution people settled here to avoid the exigencies of the sultan's rule in

Star Attraction
● **Dimitsána**

> **The three cities**
> Trípoli's name derives from the three ancient cities that once stood here ('Tri', three, 'poli', cities). They were Tegea, Mantineia and Palladium, a Roman administrative centre. The ruins of Mantineia lie north of modern Trípoli, near Levídi, while the remains of Tegea — especially the ruined Temple of Athena Alea — can be seen in the modern village of Aléa to the south.

Dimitsána

Below: a profusion of flowers
Bottom: Olympia, entrance to
the stadium

the lowlands, and once the revolution began, it served as an important stronghold. The Dimitsána library (Tues–Sat 9am–1pm), housed in the school building opposite the church, keeps papers and books from that period. As with most mountain villages in Arcadia and Kynouría, lack of opportunity has forced a large contingent of local people to leave, although many return for summer holidays.

Back on the main road, ★ **Langádia** is another village of carpenters and stonemasons. Magnificent stone-built houses spill down the steep slopes of a rocky outcrop. A few tavernas set out their tables on a terrace above a deep gorge.

OLYMPIA

Ancient ★★★ **Olympia** (Mon–Fri 8am–7pm, Sat–Sun 8.30am–3pm; museum closed Mon am), surrounded by pines and broom, lies a short way from the modern village of Olymbía, which consists predominantly of hotels, restaurants, cafés and souvenir shops. Buses run from Olympia to Trípoli, while the rail-line spur from Pýrgos gives indirect access to Pátra, Athens, and Kalámata.

The first Olympic Games were held close to the point where the Alfiós and Kládios rivers meet. The best time to sense something of the Olympic atmosphere is early morning or late afternoon, when the sound of the cicadas dominates, rather than the voices of tour guides. In early spring the pink and white blossom of the Judas and almond trees colours the spaces between the ancient columns. Allow at least half a day to see the excavated site and the museum.

THE SACRED GROVE

Although there are many columns still in place, it is worth asking for a plan with a reconstruction of the various ruined sites. The **Sacred Grove** or *altis* was surrounded by a wall, with temples to Zeus and Hera at the centre. The stadium and practice areas are situated away from the *altis*. Boxers and wrestlers prepared for their events between the colonnades of the **Gymnasium** and the **Palestra**, while the **Stadium** with its 190-m (622-ft) running course and seating was still intact enough to serve as the venue for the shot-putting events of the 2004 summer Olympics.

Huge column discs from the **Temple of Zeus** lie in the grass; when standing, these pillars reached a height of 10m (33ft). Carved marble figures adorned both pediments. This temple, the biggest at Olympia, was used for the award ceremony when the winners were presented with their olive wreaths, branches for which were clipped from a tree nearby. Prime position inside the temple was taken by one of the Seven Wonders of the ancient world, the huge seated statue of Zeus, a work by Phidias, one of the most famous sculptors of classical Greece, whose signed wine cup can be seen in the museum.

A favourite photo opportunity is the narrow-columned **Temple of Hera**, dating from the 6th and 7th centuries BC. Here at the foot of Krónio hill, the Olympic flame for the modern summer and winter games is kindled with the aid of the sun and a large parabolic mirror.

Star Attraction
● Olympia

The Olympic Stadium
A track between the Temple of Zeus and the Temple of Hera leads through a vaulted tunnel into the **Olympic Stadium**, housing up to 45,000 spectators. The stone stand was for referees and honoured guests. The start and finishing line can still be seen, establishing the length of the track as 192.27m (209.57yds).

THE MUSEUMS

With models of how Olympia looked in its prime, the ★★**Archaeological Museum** rounds off the Olympian experience. The huge central hall

Below: the Temple of Hera

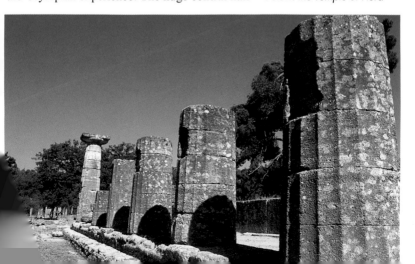

Map on pages 34–5

contains the pediments from the Temple of Zeus. The eastern pediment shows the Olympic chariot race that was won dishonestly by Pelops, who then became the ruler of the Peloponnese, while in the western composition, a serene Apollo watches riotous struggles between Lapiths and Centaurs. Other outstanding statues on display are the 4th-century BC marble Hermes by Praxiteles, which was found in the Temple of Hera, and the Nike of Paionios.

The ★**Museum of the Olympic Games** (Mon–Sat 8am–3.30pm, Sun 9am–4.30pm) in the village of Olymbía displays medals and posters and the names of winners from 1896 up to the present day.

PÁTRA

Pátra (pop. 250,000) is Greece's fourth-largest city. Ferries from Italy arrive here, creating a bustling atmosphere day and night, and many tourists use Pátra as a springboard for travelling around Greece. In Óthonos ke Amalías, Platía Tríon Symáhon and Iröön Polytehníou, streets situated close to the harbour, almost all travel requirements can be met: railway station, bus station, travel agencies and car-hire firms. The route out of town to Athens, Kalávryta and Olympia is well signposted. The large university-student population ensures that the pre-Lenten carnival (seven weeks before Easter) is particularly exuberant, with colourful processions and 'chocolate storms'. During the summer the town organises an arts festival with classical and modern Greek music, jazz and theatre; while the end of August heralds the start of the wine festival.

Pátra is halfway along the coastal rail line between Kalamáta and Athens. The futuristic suspension bridge (completed in 2004) over the Río-Andírrio straits – so large that it can be plainly seen from jets passing overhead – has greatly eased land communications with central and western Greece, including bus services to Ioánni and Delphi. Ferries leave for the Ionian island Kefaloniá, Itháki and Corfu, as well as Ita

Pátra castle

Beaches
On the way to Pátra, stop off at the beautiful beach between **Skafídia** and **Loutrá Kyllíni** (Killini Baths). The ancient Greeks and Romans came here to bathe in the warm waters (25°C/77°F) beneath the eucalyptus trees and pines. Today, however, the beaches behind the green, duney landscape are much more inviting than the spa itself.

Further up the coast is the 7-km (4-mile) sandy beach of **Kalogriá**. Behind the beach itself is one of the largest wetlands in the Balkans – yet to be protected – with a rich variety of birdlife.

5: Delphi to Metéora

Pátra – Delphi – Metéora (350km/220 miles)

Temples and monasteries are the foci of this tour. According to ancient myths, Zeus sent two eagles off in opposite directions to find the centre of the world and they collided in Delphi. Those who visit the sanctuary will appreciate its beauty and harmony and will be able to understand the credence that the ancient Greeks gave to the oracle's utterances.

The chaos of rocky pillars, pinnacles and precipices which are crowned by the monasteries of Metéora create an unforgettable impression. Allow four days to view these sights at a leisurely pace. Buses serve all the sights apart from the monasteries, which are usually at the top of arduous flights of steps.

THE STRAITS AND NAFPAKTOS

From Río, 10km (7 miles) from Pátra *(see page 54)*, vehicles cross the straits on the new **suspension bridge** in a fraction of the time taken by the old roll-on, roll-off car ferries (a few of which survive). Once on the Andírrio side, the coast road winds its way scenically along the north bank of the Gulf of Corinth beside gaunt hills, olive trees and cypresses as far as Itéa.

Map on page 56

Star Attractions
● **Archaeological Museum**
● **Náfpaktos**

Below: venerable wine barrel, Achaïa Clauss, Pátra
Bottom: Náfpaktos harbour

★Náfpaktos (pop. 7,000; 20km/12 miles), now a minor market centre and popular resort, is also a historic town. The fortified harbour and castle walls climbing a pine-clad hill were created by the Venetians; from here the combined western fleets, under the command of Don Juan of Austria, sailed out to defeat the Ottoman navy in the 1571 Battle of Lepanto. Spanish writer Cervantes lost his left arm to a Turkish canonball in the conflict, and a Spanish-erected statue at the old port honours the great man. To either side of the harbour entrance, busy with fishing boats and yachts, stretch two beaches, each with restaurants and hotels behind them: plane-shaded Grímbovo to the east, and cleaner, better-equipped Psáni to the west. Most of the town's social life takes place in the cafés and bars overlooking the old port.

GALAXIDI

Just 17km (10 miles) shy of the port of Itéa, the near-perfect Neoclassical town of **★★Galaxídi** appears suddenly as you approach from Náfpak-

tos. This was once one of Greece's major ports, but the age of steam rendered its huge schooner fleets obsolete by the 1890s, and the town has been declining gently ever since. Other than a combined maritime/folklore museum, there's nothing specific to do or see but soak up the atmosphere and appreciate the graceful architecture. Built on a ridge separating two harbours, Galaxídi is a popular, year-round weekend retreat for Athenians who stay at the boutique hotels or buy second homes. The southeasterly port is busier, with fishing boats, visiting yachts and most of the restaurants and bars.

DELPHI

Beyond Itéa, the road arcs steeply up to Hryssó where a stunning panorama opens up. Like two broad rivers, thousands of shimmering, silvery-green olive trees flow out of the deep Plistós Valley and the broad Ámfissa Plain towards the Gulf of Itéa. On the slopes of 2,500-m (8,200-ft) Mount Parnassós lies ★★★ **Delphi** (summer: Mon 8.30am–2.45pm, Tues–Sun 7.30am–6.45pm; winter:Tues–Sun 8am–5pm), the most important oracle in antiquity, and the tourist village of the same name. Allow at least a whole day to investigate the site and museum thoroughly.

MYTH AND HISTORY

This mythical centre of the ancient world and home of its most famous oracle still plays a part in Western consciousness. It was pronounced here that Oedipus would kill his father and marry his mother – thereby giving the world its most tragic hero and Freud his Oedipus complex. The utterances of the oracular priestess were deciphered by priests in exchange for money. The advice offered to kings and barren women alike was typically equivocal. The best example is the Lydian King Croesus, who was told that if he crossed the river Halys in Anatolia, 'a great empire would be destroyed'. The king assumed this predicted the destruction of the Persian empire, but in the end it was his own empire that met disaster. Over time, corruption scandals meant that trust in the oracle diminished. The Romans were more inter-

Star Attractions
● Delphi
● Galaxídi

Parnassós
One the closest mountains to Athens, Parnassós sees a substantial number of visitors – particularly in the winter when the ski station above Aráhova is busy. Two popular routes are: from Delphi to the Corycian Cave (where rites to Pan were carried out in the winter when Apollo was absent from the site below), and up to the summit of Liákoura – a more serious hike best begun from Áno Tithoréa on the northeast side of the mountain.

Mount Parnassós and Delphi

Map
on pages
56 & 58

ested in the treasures that had accumulated than in any words of wisdom. Late in the 4th century AD Delphi, along with all other pagan institutions, was proscribed by Emperor Theodosius. Earthquakes had more or less concealed the ruins before excavations began late in the 19th century.

SANCTUARY OF APOLLO

The **Sanctuary of Apollo** Ⓐ is surrounded by a natural amphitheatre of steep rock tiers. The **Sacred Way** Ⓑ leads from the entrance up through the site, passing the treasuries where pilgrims deposited their offerings, and the votive monuments by which Greek city-states expressed their wealth and power. The reconstructed **Treasury of the Athenians** Ⓒ is the best preserved of the buildings. The **Temple of Apollo** Ⓓ was the most important place within the sanctuary; several of its columns have been re-erected. The Pythian priestess dwelt in a subterranean chamber inside the temple, from where she delivered the words of the oracle. In the innermost part of the temple was the *omphalos*, the legendary stone that marked the centre of the world. Carry on past the **Theatre** Ⓔ to the **Stadium** Ⓕ, which was completed by the Romans. In these two structures the Pythian Games took place, with drama and sport in honour of Apollo. Even the Romans, it seems, had trouble with drunken sports fans: an inscription has been found forbidding spectators to bring wine into the stadium.

The oracle
Pilgrims came to Delphi to consult the Pythian soothsayer, a local woman aged over 50. After the pilgrims had submitted their questions, the soothsayer would deliver her prophecies from a tripod placed over the chasm inside the temple – these would then be 'interpreted' by one of the temple priests. It is thought that the chasm – now closed up – emitted some type of vapour that sent the soothsayer into a trance.

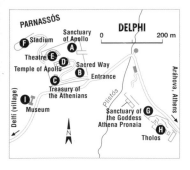

SANCTURY OF ATHENA

Below the road to Athens stands the **Sanctuary of the Goddess Athena Pronaia** Ⓖ who was worshipped as the guardian of the temple. Sections of three marble columns and a curved section of frieze from the **tholos** Ⓗ have been re-erected to form what has become the picture-postcard image of Delphi. The purpose of this ornate circular building remains unknown.

The ★★ **site museum** ❶ (summer: Mon–Fri 7.30am–6.45pm, Sat–Sun 8.30am–2.45pm; winter 8.30am–2.45pm) has been renovated and is one of the most important in Greece. A copy of the *omphalos* or navel-stone can be seen, but the real highlight is a 5th-century BC bronze figure of a victor in a chariot race. Look at the expressive details, the eyes of black onyx, the finely modelled hand and the full, proudly smiling lips.

Buses go to Itéa, Ámfissa, Aráhova and Athens.

Star Attractions
● Delphi Museum
● Ósios Loukás

Below: Ósios Loukás
Bottom: the Temple of Apollo

OSIOS LOUKAS

The best excursion from Delphi is to ★★ **Ósios Loukás Monastery** (summer: daily 8am–2pm, 4–7pm; winter: 8am–5pm), east past the hilltown of **Aráhova**, then south through Dístomo. It is famous for its 11th-century mosaics on gold backgrounds, including the *Resurrection*, the *Washing of the Apostles' Feet*, and the *Baptism of Christ*. There are no comparable mosaics in Greece, now that Néa Moní *(see page 83)* is off-limits indefinitely for restoration.

DELPHI TO TRIKALA

The journey from the Delphi area through mountains and valleys to Metéora takes a good four hours. The road passes **Ámfissa**, with its castle,

Metéora's origins

About a thousand years ago the first hermits settled in this impressive spot, and their community developed into a monks' order, which began building monasteries in the 14th century. The founder of Metéora was Athanasios Kinovitis. Both to be nearer God and to keep unwelcome guests at bay the monk built the first monastery, the Megálo Metéoron, on the highest rock. Altogether 24 monasteries were built but internal disputes, physical deterioration, and land expropriation led to most being abandoned.

Ágios Nikólaos Anapafsás

and then climbs over a saddle separating the Parnassós and Gióna ranges, before snaking down into the fertile basin around **Lamía**. After another, lower mountain ridge and **Domokós**, you reach the Thessalian plain, the breadbasket of Greece, with herons in the meadows and storks on elevated perches. Fast roads bypass the market town of Kardítsa en route to **Tríkala**, one of the more enjoyable provincial capitals, bisected by the River Lethéos, and with an old quarter under the castle hill. From Tríkala there are buses to Kalambáka, Ioánnina, Lárissa, Lamía, Athens and Thessaloníki, plus trains to Kalambáka and Vólos.

METEORA

The spectacular setting of the Metéora monasteries can be seen from a distance on the way to **Kalambáka**. The dark-grey 'stalagmites' of ★★★ **Metéora** tower almost vertically 300m (1,000ft) above the plain. Made of solidified sediment, they took shape millions of years ago as the result of tectonic plate pressures and erosion from a river flowing into the sea. A 17-km (9-mile) road loops out of Kalambáka and passes the perched **monasteries**, with their vivid frescoes. Of the original 24, only eight survive, of which six are inhabited (hours vary, but each is open 9am–2pm, plus late afternoon hours for the more popular ones). Women should wear long skirts and cover their shoulders and men must wear long trousers.

The first monastery after **Kastráki** village (the best place to stay overnight), ★★ **Agíou Nikoláou Anapafsá**, with 16th-century frescoes, is reached, like most of them, by a long flight of steps. The biggest and highest monastery, ★★ **Megálou Meteórou**, offers a rich museum rather than the most significant frescoes, while its neighbour **Varláam** has more frescoes. ★★ **Roussanoú**, across the canyon, enjoys the most spectacular pinnacle-top setting and slightly later but noteworthy frescoes, while ★ **Ayías Triádhos** has more wall-art and the voluble monk, Ioannis.

Public transport services for Kalambáka are essentially identical to Tríkala's.

6: Epirus

Kalambáka – Métsovo – Ioánnina – Víkos Gorge – Kastoriá (400km/250 miles)

Even for a regular visitor to Greece, the northwest is likely to be new territory, with steep mountains and wooded valleys as far as the eye can see. The Píndos Mountains in the region of Epirus, contains the country's second and third loftiest peaks. Greece's highest drivable pass, the Katára, cuts through dense coniferous forests where wolves and bears still roam. Beyond a few Ottoman minarets, the mountains close off the horizon of the lively lakeside town of Ioánnina; just north lies the remote region of Zagóri, with some of its stone-built villages teetering on the edge of the 1,000-m (3,250-ft) deep Víkos Gorge. The final destination for this tour is the mountain town of Kónitsa. Allow at least four days, although serious walkers will want to stay longer in this spectacular region

METSOVO

A winding road leaves Kalambáka in the direction of Ioánnina, negotiating the **Katára Pass**, which serves as a natural border between Thessaly and Epirus. (A bit further north towards Grevená you'll be able to access the fast Via

Map on page 62

Star Attraction
● **Metéora**

Below: Métsovo
Bottom: on Ioánnina Kástro

Map below

Egnatia expressway to Métsovo and Ioánnina, set to open in 2006.) The town of ★**Métsovo** covers a slope facing the south Píndos summit of Peristéri, which is carpeted by a thick layer of snow, sometimes 2m (6ft) deep, from December to April; accordingly there is a small, rather creaky ski centre (four runs, two lifts) just outside town. The local stone houses are solidly built, though the traditional schist roofs have vanished in favour of ugly tiles. Souvenir shops display kitsch carved woodwork and more worthwhile woven goods.

THE TOSITSA MUSEUM

Follow copious signs to the ★★**Tosítsa Museum** (Fri–Wed 9.30am–1.30pm, 4–6pm), an unusual folk museum housed in a traditional Epirot mansion, the restored home of the Tositsa family *(see next page)*. The old bread oven dominates the kitchen, with saucepans and frying pans hang-

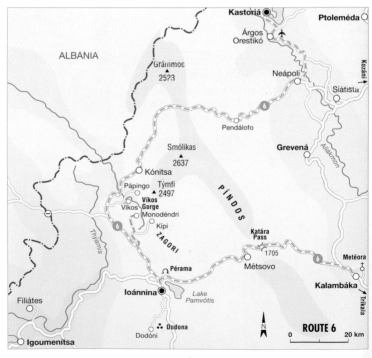

ing from the wall above. One reception room is comfortably furnished with large sofas, red kilims and thick cushions. On the first floor, low copper tables and eastern-style benches occupy the parlour. It may be possible to glance inside the cupboards to see the beautiful silver necklaces.

The Tositsa and Averoff families have been responsible for the continuation of Métsovo's traditional lifestyle. In the 1930s the politician Evangelos Averof,concerned that the inhabitants of his home town were emigrating to the cities, managed to persuade Baron Mihaïl Tositsa, a wealthy Metsovot banker living in Switzerland, to make a bequest to Métsovo. With this, the woodworking industry was rejuvenated, a cheese-making factory established and a bull of exceptional pedigree bought to improve the quality of the cattle.

IOANNINA

★ **Ioánnina** (pop. 100,000 is the administrative centre of Epirus, a major university and garrison town, and one of Greece's fastest-growing cities. The modern sprawl envelopes the town's smallish historic bazaar, where a few traditional tradesmen – tailors, cobblers, metal-workers – are now outnumbered by souvenir stalls. Among the latter, the silversmiths carry on a centuries-old small industry and have a reasonable reputation.

The ★★ **Kástro** or medieval walled town is partly a legacy of Ali Pasha, a ruthless Albanian despot who ruled here from 1788–1821, bringing a measure of prosperity but finally defying the sultan once too often. An Ottoman army was sent to besiege Ioánnina; Ali fled to the small inhabited island across Lake Pamvótida, where his attackers found and killed him. Turkish rule in this area ended only in February 1913. The ★★ **Aslan Pasha Mosque**, now the town **museum** (summer: daily 8am–8.30pm; winter: 9am–3pm), has an interesting ethnographic collection.

Boats to the island leave every hour from the landing stage below the *kástro*. The island, blissfully car-free, has several little monasteries besides the one (Ágios Pandelímon) where Ali

Star Attractions
- **Tosítsa Museum**
- **Ioánnina**
- **Aslan Pasha Mosque**

The Píndos
Métsovo makes a good base for touring the Píndos National Park north of the Katáras Pass. In the park rare animals are still being hunted by over-anxious shepherds or poachers, despite their protected species status. In 1994 an EU-sponsored project was initiated to try to save the last remaining brown bears, thought to number only 120. Walkers need not be too concerned as the bears are extremely shy and are unlikely to emerge from their lairs.

There are regular buses from Métsovo serving Ioánnina and Kalambáka.

Tosítsa Museum costumes

Map on page 102

Pasha hid and was killed. The most interesting is **Ágiou Nikoláou Filanthropinón**, whose church contains well-preserved frescoes of the Life of Christ dating from 1292.

Ioánnina has two bus stations: on Zozimádou for Athens, Thessaloníki, Igoumenítsa and Zagóri, and on Bizaníou for Dodóni.

Below: Dodóni theatre
Bottom: the Víkos Gorge

DODONI

★★ **Dodóni**, 22 km (14 miles) southwest of Ioánnina, is the site of the oldest oracle in Greece, dating from the 2nd millenium BC. Olympias, mother of Alexander the Great, was the daughter of an Epirot king who ruled locally in the 4th century BC. A sacred oak dedicated to Zeus once stood here, and the rustling leaves were used by the priestesses to answer pilgrims' questions. The steeply tiered semi-circular **theatre** (daily 8am–5pm) dates from the 3rd century BC, but was meticulously restored in the late 19th century. Finds from Dodoni are in Ioánnina's Archaeological Museum (currently closed for renovation).

PERAMA

A grotto with bizarrely shaped stalagmites and stalactites was discovered during World War II at ★ **Pérama**, 4km (2½ miles) east of Ioánnina. The

cave system is claimed to be Greece's largest. There is a 45-minute tour of the cave (summer: daily 8am–8pm; winter 8am–sunset).

ZAGORI

Forty-six small, beautiful villages are tucked away in the remote mountain region of **Zagóri**. The *zagorohória*, as they are called, are architecturally homogenous, constructed from pale local limestone and roofed in flat schist slabs. The best preserved and most frequently visited communities are all close to the Víkos Gorge, which ties with the Samarian Gorge in Crete as Greece's longest, and is the focus of the **Víkos–Aöós National Park**. Little ★ **Monodéndri** is the most popular jumping-off point to traverse the gorge floor *(see margin box)*, but hikers also start from nearby Vítsa. They finish either in Víkos village (the shortest walk), or continue to busier **Megálo Pápingo** or **Mikró Pápingo**, all with ample food and lodging. An extra day around the Pápingos to explore the Dragon Lake of Mount Gamíla, also within the park boundaries, is recommended.

KONITSA AND MOUNT SMOLIKAS

An arched bridge soaring over the Aöós River marks your approach to **Kónitsa**. Both the Aöós and the Voïdomatis rivers are favourite spots for white-water kayaking and canoeing, and two local centres provide expertise and equipment. Walkers can go a considerable way up the ★ **Aöós Gorge**, the favourite target being the monastery of Stomíou. Kónitsa is the closest town to **Mount Smólikas**, second highest peak in Greece (2,637m/8,651ft); a bus service takes you to **Paleosélli**, the trailhead village, with a new alpine refuge a couple of hours' walk above. The large village of **Pendálofos** en route to Kastoriá marks the transition to the region of Macedonia, and makes a good meal stop. Shortly beyond, at the junction settlement of Neápoli, the busiest road goes north to the lakeside town of Kastoriá, famous for its frescoed Byzantine churches.

Star Attractions
● **Dodóni**
● **The Víkos Gorge**

> ### The Víkos Gorge
> The splendid ★★ Víkos Gorge is a wonderful sight. For some 10km (7 miles) the river has furrowed 1,000m (3,250ft) deep into the reddish-grey rock. The limestone strata here are stacked in reef-like formations, often eroded into palisades or pinnacles. The view from Oxiá, the rock balcony near Monodéndri, is breathtaking. The rocks drop 400m (1,300ft) vertically down into the valley, the deeply fissured Mégas Lákkos or Big Trench, which then opens out into the gorge opposite. The river itself is hidden at the foot of the valley among pines and beeches. Many hardy souls make the seven-hour trek through the gorge between Monodéndri and the spectacularly beautiful village of Pápingo where they stay overnight.

Pérama

Map below

7: Macedonia

Kastoriá – Vergína – Thessaloníki (230km/140 miles)

The face of Macedonia changes as this route heads east. Mountains and lakes characterise the west, with its focus the historic, picturesque town of Kastoriá on the shores of Lake Orestiáda. On the road to Kozáni, the next provincial capital, beech-covered hillsides give way to gently rolling countryside of grain fields and peach orchards. Véria can offer an old quarter, a mix of crumbling mosques and frescoed churches, and an escarpment setting. Nearby is a site that shouldn't be missed: the tomb of Philip II, king of ancient Macedonia, and other members of his dynasty, on the outskirts of the village of Vergína.

Kastoría

Thessaloníki *(see pages 70–73)* with a harbour, airport, trade fair and cultural events is northern Greece's window on the world. Bus services between Thessaloníki and other Macedonian towns are good, but a car gives more freedom. The route can be covered easily in two days.

KASTORIA

The town of ★ **Kastoriá** (pop. 30,000) is spread over a hill on a peninsula that juts out into Lake Orestiáda. The town centre of this historic trading centre is a labyrinth of narrow alleys covering the hilly promontory. Kastoriá is known worldwide for its furs, and the approaches to town are lined with signboards in Cyrillic pitching the goods to Russian wheeler-dealers.

ROUTE 7

Of more enduring interest are Kastoriá's Byzantine churches and remaining Ottoman houses, concentrated in the hillside quarter of **Dóltso**. The town has dozens of churches, and the **Byzantine Museum** (Tues–Sun 8.30am–3pm), which houses a collection of vivid icons dating back to the 13th century, is the place to find a guide to admit you to the best ones.

ANCIENT CHURCHES

Byzantine churches are scattered fairly evenly across the old town. They are generally lit only dimly, by natural light filtering through tiny windows, as strong sunshine or artificial light would soon fade the frescoes. The ★★**Panagía Koumbelidikí**, dating from the 10th–15th centuries, takes its name from its cylindrical dome-drum (*kübe* in Turkish), and preserves a rare, expressive fresco of the Holy Trinity. ★**Ágii Anárgyri**, a triple-naved basilica, has an 11th-century geometrically-patterned brick facade; some of its frescoes, in particular the soldier-saints Ágios Dimítrios and Ághios Geórgios, have been cleaned. Nearby ★**Ágios Stéfanos** has no noteworthy frescoes, but does retain a *gynekonítis* (a wooden gallery for women) upstairs. The 12th-century ★★**Ágios Nikólaos Kaznítzi** had its vivid frescoes cleaned during the 1980s; while the oldest church in the town, ★★**Taxiárhes tís Mitropóleos**, dates from the 9th century, and contains more striking frescoes, as well as the tomb of nationalist warrior Pavlos Melas.

A tour of the churches can be combined with a stroll along the lakeside quay; the cafés on the promenade provide coffee and pastries, plus a superb view across the lake to the mountains.

SIATISTA AND VERIA

Kastoriá is connected by bus to Kozáni, Athens and Thessaloníki; there are also daily flights to Athens. With your own transport, take the road out of Kastoriá first to Neápoli, then to **Siátista**, another historic furriers' town which also has a

Star Attraction
● Panagía Koumbelidikí

Macedonia
It can be difficult for visitors to understand how feelings can run so high over a name. When the Yugoslav republic of Macedonia declared independence in 1991 it adopted the name Macedonia and put the star of Vergína on it flag. This inflamed right-wing Greek nationalists who promptly demanded that the new republic adopt a different name and symbol (claiming that 'Macedonia is Greek' – a slogan seen everywhere at the time). Largely unsupported by the international community, Greece imposed a unilateral economic boycott – only lifted in 1995 – and pressured the state into adopting the interim name of Former Yugoslav Republic of Macedonia (FYROM).

Panagía Koumbelidikí

Map on page 66

Vergína treasures
The gold and silver unearthed during the excavations at Vergína constitute one of the richest hoards ever found in Greece. Among the pieces was a gold casket with a 16-pointed star, the emblem of Philip II's dynasty, on its lid, a gold oak-leaf wreath, and a silver vase containing the ashes of the son of Alexander the Great.

The palace ruins, Pella

handful of well-preserved, 18th-century mansion-museums that can be visited. Bypass charmless Kozáni and carry on to **Véria** (pop. 30,000). In spring, hundreds of peach trees blossom around this provincial capital, which was visited twice by the Apostle Paul. A shrine has been built on the site where he supposedly delivered his homilies. During the reign of the Roman emperor Diocletian, Véria was one of Macedonia's most important towns, and the **Archaeological Museum** displays many exhibits from Hellenic and Roman times. Hidden away in the old town are a number of Byzantine churches, the 14th-century **Anastáseos** (Resurrection) being the most notable of these because of its cleaned frescoes. Opposite the old cathedral, its truncated minaret a legacy of the time it was used as a mosque, stands an ancient plane tree where the town's archbishop was hanged in 1430. The former ravine-bank quarter of **Barboúta**, home to nearly 1,000 Jews until 1943, is being steadily restored; you can still see the old **synagogue**.

From Véria there are trains to Thessaloníki and buses to Vergína, Kozáni and Thessaloníki. The road journey to Thessaloníki (230km/140 miles) is fast, but before you go, detour to Vergína.

VERGINA

★★★ **Ancient Vergína** is only 15km (9 miles) from Véria. The most impressive site here is a complex of royal tombs, found by the archaeologist Manolis Andronikos inside a tumulus in November 1977. Two of the four tombs had been plundered, probably in antiquity, although one of them contained a beautiful mural. However, two other nearby tombs were intact. The gold and silver articles found in one, and the skeleton itself, bearing the marks of wounds that Philip II, the father of Alexander the Great, is known to have received, led Andronikos to conclude that this was the grave of that particular Macedonian king, and that 'Vergína' (actually the name of the adjacent modern village) was in fact ancient Aegae. Philip II had been buried in Aegae in 336BC, although at that time Pella, further north, was the Macedonian capital. The oracle at Delphi had predicted the end of the dynasty if its kings were not buried in Vergína – as indeed happened when Alexander the Great died in Mesopotamia. His son, Alexander IV, was murdered when an adolescent, and his bones were found in a silver container in the remaining untouched tomb.

The **Royal Tombs**, along with their grave finds, form the centrepiece of an **underground museum** (summer: Mon 12.30–7pm, Tues–Sun 8am–7pm; winter: closes at 5pm), all displayed impeccably in a climate-controlled environment. The imposing facades of the tombs, safe behind heavy glass, retain traces of pigment on their friezes. Among the contents is the gold ossuary for the bones of Philip II, embossed with the 16-pointed 'Star of Vergína', apparently the symbol of the dynasty.

South of the modern village of Vergína, you can also visit a cluster of five more tombs, a generation older than the preceding ones, and the site of **Palatítsia**, which was probably a 3rd-century BC summer residence for the last great Macedonian king, Antigonus Gonatus. Here, too, are a few seating rows from the theatre where Philip is said to have been assassinated in 336 BC. But none of this can really compare with the riches of the Royal Tombs.

Star Attraction
● **Vergína**

Below: mosaic floor, Pella
Bottom: lion hunt, Pella

Map on page 71

8: Thessaloníki

Thessaloníki (pop. 1 million) is Greece's second city and administrative centre of the Macedonia and Thrace regions. It sprawls between the head of the Thermaic Gulf and the low hills just inland, with the Áxios (Vardar) River just west. Thessaloníki is an ideal place to study the development of Byzantine church architecture, and to do some shopping in the expensive boutiques lining Tsimiskí Street. One of the best places to soak up a more traditional commercial atmosphere is the ★ **covered market (Modiáno) ❶** (Mon–Sat until 2.30pm). The market halls and the open bazaar in the lanes around it are replete with fishmongers, butchers' stalls and tables piled high with fruit and vegetables; inside, especially near the west gate, some atmospheric *ouzerís* survive.

History

Founded in 315BC, Thessaloníki was named after the half-sister of Alexander the Great and wife of Kassander, the city's founder. From 170BC Thessaloníki was the capital of the Roman province of Macedonia and served as an important staging post on the Via Egnatia, the road which linked Rome with Constantinople. The town suffered during the Middle Ages, first at the hands of the Arabs and later the Normans. In 1430 the Turks attacked and killed or enslaved many Greeks, remaining in control until 1912, but they were not the last occupying forces. During World War II the Germans destroyed the city's Jewish community. This had been one of the largest in Europe, resident in the city since the turn of the 16th century.

BYZANTINE MONUMENTS

Thessaloníki was for centuries one of the major cities of the Byzantine and Ottoman empires, and many traces of these periods remain. The ★ **White Tower ❷** is easy to find and makes a good starting point. Built by the Byzantines but adapted by the Ottomans, it formed part of the seafront town wall. One of its early functions was as a prison, and after the massacre of the Janissaries in 1826 it earned the name 'Bloody Tower'. It houses a museum of medieval art (closed until 2006). Art treasures are also found behind the simple brick facade of the ★★ **Agía Sofía ❸**. In the dome is a mosaic of the Ascenscion, while in the apse is an equally fine 10th-century mosaic of the Virgin Enthroned.

The White Tower

ROMAN AND OTTOMAN THESSALONIKI

The Roman ★ **Arch of Galerius ❹**, the remains of a larger triumphal arcade, was built in AD297 by Emperor Galerius to commemorate his victory over the Persians; the marble reliefs of battles and processions are particularly interesting. The arch was originally linked to the ★★ **Rotónda ❺**

(Tues–Fri 8am–7pm, Sat–Sun 8.30am–3pm). The biggest circular building in Europe after the Pantheon in Rome, it was built in AD306, probably as a mausoleum for Emperor Galerius, but in the 5th century it was converted into the church of Ágios Geórgios, and adorned with superb mosaics – although some will be hidden by scaffolding until 2006. The minaret alongside dates from its time as a mosque. The remains of the **Roman Agora** ❻ lie a few blocks northwest, although several decades of excavation have turned up little other than foundations, tesselated floor and a reconstructed odeon. Nearby are two Turkish **hamams** (one converted to a bar and summer cinema), and the **Hamza Bey mosque** and **Bezesteni** (covered market), straddling the Roman road that passed through here en route to Byzantium.

AGIOS DIMITRIOS AND SURROUNDINGS

Just uphill from the Agora stands ★★**Ágios Dimítrios** ❼ (Mon 1.30–7.30pm, Tues–Sun 8am–7.30pm), the largest church in Greece. It is dedicated to St Dimitrios, the town's patron

Star Attractions
- **Agía Sofía**
- **Rotónda**
- **Ágios Dimítrios**

The Rotónda

Map
on page
71

*Below: sunset over Thessaloníki harbour
Below: the tomb of Ágios Dimítrios*

saint, a Roman officer who lost favour with the Emperor Diocletian when he embraced Christianity. He was imprisoned and later speared to death. A 5th-century chapel was said to have stood on the site of his prison cell. The basilica was almost entirely rebuilt after the great fire of 1917 which destroyed much of the town. Precious mosaics, including four from the 7th century, the earliest in Greece, were rescued and incorporated in the new church. Dimitrios is greatly revered by the Thessalonians, not least because in 1912 the Ottomans left Thessaloníki on his feast-day and the Germans withdrew on the same day in 1944.

On one edge of a park a few blocks downhill stands 11th-century **Panagía Halkéon** ❽ (open mornings), a fine example of a Byzantine cruciform triple-domed basilica. On the opposite side of the park is 5th-century **Panagía Ahiropíitos**, the oldest church in the city, distinguished by ornate interior colonnades with a few surviving mosaics under their arches.

THE SEAFRONT

★**Platía Aristotélous** ❾, across Via Egnatia (the Roman road), opens out to the sea at its far end. The bar in the Electra Palace Hotel, plus the *ouzerís* Tottis and Aristotelous on the opposite side of the plaza, are favourite meetings places,

as are the growing number of cafés on Níkis, the quayside street on either side of Aristotélous.

THE UPPER TOWN

There's a superb view over Thessaloníki and the Thermaic Gulf from the ★ **Upper Town ❿**, comprising the Kástra and Eptapyrgío quarters . This district can be reached by bus from the Platía Eléftherias; alight at Eptapyrgío, where parts of the Byzantine wall are still in place. At the summit, the former prison of **Yediküle** is now a museum. Just below, in Kástra, stands the 14th-century **Vlatádon Monastery ⓫** (7.30–11am, 4–7pm), with a romantic courtyard. More noteworthy artistically is the little church of **Ósios Davíd** nearby, with a fine mosaic of a beardless Christ and two prophets. On your way down through Kástra, detour to 14th-century **Ágios Nikólaos Orfanós** (Tues–Sun 8.45am–2.45pm), with the best frescoes in the city.

MUSEUMS

The ★★ **Archaeological Museum ⓬** (summer: Mon 12.30–7pm, Tues–Sun 8am–7pm; winter: Mon 10.30am–5pm, Tues–Sun 8.30am–3pm) displays northern Greece's major archaeological finds, ranging from prehistoric vases to Roman mosaic floors. Many of the richest gravegoods have been sent back to the museum at Vergína, but what's left is still impressive. Two other worthwhile museums are the **Jewish Museum** (Tues–Fri and Sun 11am–2pm, Wed–Thur 5–8pm), at Ayíou Miná 13, tracing the history of what was (until 1944) one of Europe's largest Jewish communities; and the **Museum of Byzantine Culture** (hours as for Archaeological Museum, above) at Stratoú 2, which features wall paintings from early Christian tombs.

In addition to Thessaloníki's extensive connections to other Greek destinations, there are conventional ferries to Lésvos, Híos and Iráklio; catamarans serve some of the northern Sporádes in summer.

Star Attraction
● **Archaeological Museum**

Thessaloníki by Night
The Ladádika quarter ⓭ to the west of Platía Eléftherias shows another side of Thessaloníki. By day tiny shops sell coffee and flour; by night smart bars attract young people who come to drink wine and listen to contemporary music (hip-hop, techno, etc.), mostly taped. The renovated facades complement the pretty but decaying houses alongside. Once the city's red-light district, the area is now fashionable, having successfully preserved some of its old vitality.

Another place for an evening's entertainment, but best reached by taxi, is O Mýlos. This former mill has been converted into restaurants, concert venues, exhibition rooms, an open-air cinema and a theatre.

Head of a philosopher, Thessaloníki Museum

Map
below

9: Mount Áthos

**Thessaloníki – Sithonía – Mount Áthos (250km/
155 miles)**

*One of Sithonía's
superb beaches*

In legend, the three-pronged Halkidikí peninsula
was formed during a battle between the ancient
gods and their adversaries, the Titans. The sea god
Poseidon is said to have lost his trident in the
struggle when the Titan Athos flung a huge boul-
der, which got impaled on one of the prongs – it's
still there, as the peak of Mount Áthos. The three
sub-peninsulas, Kassándra, Sithonía and Áthos,
are easily reached by car, bus or bicycle from
Thessaloníki. Áthos is subject to a special regime
(see page 76), but Sithonía and Kassándra make
ideal weekend getaways, and are treated as such
by Thessalonians. In Thessaloníki, buses from
a station at Karakássi 68 leave for all points on
Halkidikí.

HALKIDIKI

Many place-names on ★★ **Halkidikí** carry the pre-
fix 'Néa' or 'Néos', meaning 'new'. In 1923, over
one million Greeks were expelled from their
homes in Asia Minor after the disastrous war
against Turkey, and many started new lives here,
repopulating an area that had lain largely deso-

late after reprisals for its futile participation in the 1821 revolution. Little is left to show the important role Halkidikí played in Classical times, when local colonies of various southern Greek cities served as important battlefields during the Peloponnesian War between Athens and Sparta. Before that, the region was the scene of a major shipwreck and naval defeat for the Persians fleet under Xerxes.

However, the hilltop ruins of 5th-century BC ★ **ancient Olynthos** have survived on the road between Kassándra and Sithonía, and reward a visit. Just inland from Néa Kalikrátia, evidence of Halkidikí's millennial habitation sufaced at the **Grotto of Kókkines Pétres** (daily 9am–sunset; guided tour) near Petrálona village. Here, in 1959, among reddish stalagmites and animal bones, archaeologists discovered the skull of a Neanderthal man, which was reckoned to be more than 200,000 years old; a museum by the cave documents the finds.

KASSANDRA AND SITHONIA

★ **Kassándra** has more settlements than Sithonía – the most attractive being the old stone villages of **Áfytos** and **Kállandra** – and also a greater degree of tourist commercialisation, with megahotel complexes, phalanxes of weekend villas, lots of watersports facilities, and two established summer festivals at Sáni and Sivíri.

However, the countryside, with its pine forests and olive groves, is arguably prettier on ★★ **Sithonía**, as are the beaches. Once past the main west-coast town of **Néos Marmarás** (130km/80 miles) and the ostentatious hotels at Pórto Cárras, there are more low-key resorts such as Toróni, with a good beach and minor archaeological site; and ★ **Pórto Koufós** (160km/100 miles), with its perfect, landlocked harbour. Rounding the tip of the peninsula to the east coast, you will find more excellent beaches between **Sykiá** and **Sárti**. The best and most scenic of these beaches is at ★★ **Kalamítsi**, with a scuba-diving centre as an added bonus.

Star Attractions
- Halkidikí
- Sithonía peninsula
- Kalamítsi

Equal access
The ambiguous status of Áthos as an independent monastic republic within the state of Greece has, up until now, seen off any challenge to its long-standing policies of banning access to women and restricting the numbers of men it admits. However, these rules fall foul of two ideals enshrined in European law: gender equality and freedom of passage for EU citizens. The Orthodox Church are still holding out against change, but there have been challenges in the courts on both counts – it remains to be seen which side will eventually win.

A vivid display

Map on page 74

Map on page 74

Áthos permits

Men wishing to visit Mount Áthos should fax a copy of their passport or EU ID to the **Pilgrims' Office** (*Grafío Proskynitón Agíou Órous*) in **Thessaloniki** (tel: 2310 861 611, fax: 2310 861 811; no walk-ins). Ten permits a day are issued to non-Orthodox. You will be issued with a reservation confirmation valid for residence on Áthos for up to four days, specifying a date for entry. This is not the permit proper but with a slip, to be exchanged for a *diamonitírion* in Ouranoúpoli. You can have the slip posted or faxed or you can go to the office in person: Konstandinou Karamanlí 14, 1st Floor, east of Thessaloníki University (Mon–Fri 9am–2pm, Sat 10am–noon, closed Sun and major holy days).

Dionysíou Monastery

ATHOS AND ITS MONASTERIES

When the weather is fine, the outline of majestic ★★★ **Mount Áthos** (2,033m/6,670ft) will be clearly visible from Sithonía. The peninsula of which it is the summit is a semi-autonomous monastic republic, its status set forth in the Greek constitution. Only men may actually set foot on it *(see box)*, by the terms of a millennium-old edict banning all higher female animals (except a few cats). Hermit-monks first gravitated to the mountain during the 7th century; under the protection and patronage of the Byzantine emperor, the community had grown to about 20,000 by the 15th century. Today there are 20 surviving monasteries, plus various smaller settlements, which together are home to about 2,000 monks – many of them foreign, well educated, and rather fanatical.

Excursions by boat to Áthos for families and couples leave from **Órmos Panagías** and ★ **Ouranópoli**, the last secular settlement before the border. The cruise boats follow the southwest-facing Athonite coastline some 500m/yds offshore, still close enough for many of the impressive monasteries to be seen. The most striking ones are **Símonos Pétras**, looking like a Tibetan lamasery; **Osíou Grigoríou**, surrounded on three sides by the sea; and **Ayíou Pandelímonos**, which betrays the traditionally Russian origins of its monks with a forest of onion-domes.

10: Mount Olympus and Pílion

**Thessaloníki – Mount Olympus – Mount Pílion
(240km/150 miles)**

Map below

Spend a day at beaches of the Thermaic Gulf, at the foot of Mount Olympus (Óros Ólymbos) – it is only an hour from Thessaloníki; enjoy the company of the gods at the top of Mount Olympus. After that, try Mount Pílion, with its unusual villages, burgeoning greenery and secluded bays. Five days is the minimum for this tour; you'll need a car (rentable in Vólos) to see Ambelákia and the Pílion peninsula properly, but other points of interest lie along principal bus and train lines.

Star Attractions
● Mount Olympus
● Mount Áthos

THERMAIC GULF BEACHES

The first staging post is **Korinós** with a fine sandy beach. The village is accessed by the old coast road, leaving the newer motorway at Néa Agathoúpoli. There are several hotels by the shore, and families are welcome. Those in search of a little more excitement can travel a further 5km (3 miles) down the road to **Paralía**. The beach is narrower, but there are tavernas, music clubs and generally more going on.

MOUNT OLYMPUS

A short journey from the coast brings one to the seat of the gods. Of Olympus' nine recognised peaks, all are above 2,600m (8,528ft), with **Mýtikas**, the loftiest, reaching 2,917m (9,567ft). Impressed by its height and rapid climb from the sea, the ancient Greeks believed ★★ **Mount Olympus** to be the home of the gods. The summits are often shrouded in mist and clouds and, when Zeus wants, he can send down thunder and lightning. The non-technical climbing season is June to October, with the most stable, clear conditions in autumn.

Paths lead up into the densely wooded mountains from **Litóhoro**, once a place

Map on page 77

The Vale of Témbi
Beyond Platamónas, the motorway leaves the coast and parallels the railway and river through the ★ **Vale of Témbi**. Apollo once lived in the lush gorge, as did the nymph Daphne. The god lusted after her, and Daphne called on her father, the river-god Pineios, to save her. This he did by turning her into a laurel tree. Willows, planes and laurels border the River Piniós. Beside the river is a sign marked Agía Paraskeví; you can walk or take a boat through the gorge from here.

tuberculosis patients were sent for healthy air, and now the base camp for the climb. An 18-km (11-mile) road, paved the first 11km (7 miles), winds up to the trailhead at **Prióna** (1,100m/3,600ft; take a taxi from Litóhoro) where the ascent to the top begins in earnest; roughly halfway is the staffed alpine refuge of **Spílios Agápitos**. From there it is possible to make it to the top and back in one day, but it's better to make a half-circle around the alpine zone, emerging at the **Gortsiá** trail head. From there, backtrack slightly on the road to **Agíou Dionysíou monastery**, burned in 1943 but still impressive, and begin the four-hour return to Litóhoro on the E4 trail through the **Mavrólongos** canyon, hollowed out by the swift-flowing Enipéfs River.

PLATAMONAS

The resort of ★ **Platamónas** lies at the point where the Olympus foothills crowd the sea; always a strategic narrows, and today marking the transition from Macedonia to Thessaly, it probably had some sort of fortification long before the Latin crusaders built the present **castle** in 1204. This is the setting for a July–August festival; the railway tunnel has been bored right under it. The camp-sites below the castle get busy in summer.

Mount Olympus

THE THESSALIAN PLAIN

As soon as the Vale of Témbi opens out into the Thessalian plain, a road leads off from the motorway to ★ **Ambelákia**. With its cobbled streets and plane-shaded square with grills and *kafenía*, it makes an excellent (if atypical) introduction to the region. Dye works and a spinning mill brought prosperity to the village during the 18th century, and several dozen *arhondiká* (traditional mansions) bear witness to Ambelákia's heyday. Many have crumbled since World War II, while others have been restored. That of the textile magnate Georgios Mavros is now a ★★ **museum** (Tues–Sat 8.45am–3pm, Sun 9.30am–2.30pm). Colourful naive wall paintings are the outstanding features of the upper storey, while the ground-floor utility quarters are stone-floored and solidly rustic.

By using the new motorway, you can bypass the dull military town of Lárissa and head towards Vólos. From the Aerinó exit, however, it's worth detouring west 12km (8 miles) to one of the most important surviving rural monuments in Greece: the Bektashi dervish 'monastery', known as the ★ **Tekkés Farsálon**, above the village of Lefkógia. Returning to the motorway and heading east on a smaller divided highway brigns you finally to **Vólos**, a port made lively by its student population and famous *tsipourádika*. With good rail, bus and ferry services, it is the jumping-off point for Mount Pílion and the Sporádes islands.

THE PILION PENINSULA

In ancient mythology, the mountainous, verdant ★★ **Pílion Peninsula** was home of the centaurs, beasts said to be half-man, half-horse, skilled in healing with herbal potions and poultices. The place where Asklepios of Trikke (now Trikala) came to study with them is now a weekend haven for Athenians and Thessalonians. A winding 140-km (87-mile) loop through one of Greece's most densely forested landscapes will take at least two days. Having returned to Vólos, Athens is about a four-hour drive away, Thessaloníki a bit less.

Star Attractions
• **Mount Pílion**
• **Ambelákia Museum**

Below: naive painting, Ambelákia Museum
Bottom: a Pílion beach

Map
on page
77

Pílion specialities

Walking in Pilion

With its well-developed system of footpaths (many of them restored traditional routes), Pilion is one of the best places for mountain walking in Greece. There are books and maps (of varying accuracy) available in Athens or the UK. There are also guided tours run by various agencies – enquire in Vólos or Ágios Ioánnis.

The easiest goal is ★★**Makrinítsa** (17km/10 miles from Vólos), draped over steep slopes overlooking the Pagasitic Gulf. Cars must be left in a parking lot on the outskirts. Once past rows of shops peddling kitsch souvenirs, candied nuts and honey, you're in one of the densest surviving collections of traditional Pílion houses. Their roofs and lath-and-plaster upper storeys protrude above two lower floors of local stone. Shutters of dark wood contrast with white plaster walls, often with ornamental arabesques of paint-swirls. These impressive *arhondiká* testify to the wealth engendered by 18th-century silk production. A narrow lane leads to the village square, shaded by spring-nurtured plane trees. Beyond the little church, its apse carved in intricate relief, is an old *kafenío* with frescoes by Greece's premier primitive artist, Theofilos Hatzimihaïl (1873–1934).

THE LOOP TOUR

Return to the main trans-peninsula road at Portariá and climb via spectacular bends to **Hánia** (30km/20 miles), a roadside sequence of hotels and tavernas that only comes to life in winter when the small ski resort nearby at **Agriólefkes** functions. From the 1551-m/5,080-ft peak, the slopes of Pílion drop steeply to white-sand Aegean beaches. In spring, cherry and apple orchards are a mass of white and pink blossoms.

Heading east at a Y-fork, you soon reach **Kissós**, with a typical Pílion church on the tiered plaza, an 18th-century basilica with an ornate icon screen and dark frescoes. A side road descends to popular beaches either side of **Ágios Ioánnis**, the busiest resort on this coast. Back on the main road, you pass **Tsangarádha**, spread over ridges that plunge to more beaches, such as ★**Mylopótamos** with its famous rock arch. The clockwise circuit continues south, then west through Mediterranean vegetation to emerge at **Miliés**, terminus of a narrow-gauge, steam-train from Áno Lehónia at weekends. The busiest road rejoins the Pagasitic Gulf at **Kalá Nerá**, and the coast road leads west back to Vólos (140km/87 miles).

11: The Eastern Aegean

In the eastern Aegean, within sight of the Turkish coast, lie three of the largest islands. All have airports and can be reached by ferry from Piraeus and northern Greece; there are also inter-island ferry services from the Dodecanese and Cyclades.

LESVOS

Lésvos, the third largest Greek island after Crete and Évvia, is known for its vast olive groves, ouzo production, salted sardines, and for a special kind of love. Surviving fragments of the erotic work of local 6th-century BC poetess Sappho can be construed as being addressed to other women. Consequently, **Skála Eressoú** (near ancient Eressos, Sappho's hometown) has become a pilgrimage spot for lesbians. The enormous beach here is one of Lésvos' best.

The island is also known by the name of the bustling capital, ★ **Mytilíni**. The skyline is dominated by the silver dome of the church of Ágios Therápon, across from which is a worthwhile ecclesiastical museum. Other attractions include the originally Byzantine **fortress** on the headland

Map below

Star Attraction
● Makrinítsa

Mytilíni castle

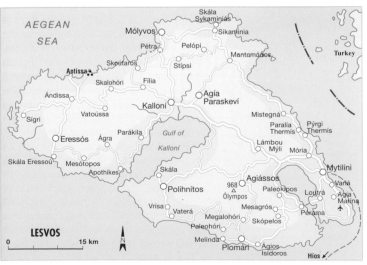

AEGEAN SEA

Skála Sykaminiás
Sikaminia
Mólyvos
Pétra
Pelópi
Skoútaros
Mantamádos
Stípsi
Antissa
Skalohóri
Fília
Ándissa
Agía Paraskeví
Kalloní
Vatoússa
Mistegná
Sígri
Paralía Thermís
Pýrgi Thermís
Parákila
Gulf of
Eressós
Ágra
Kalloní
Lámbou Mýli
Mória
Skála Eressoú
Mesótopos
Apothíkes
Skála
Mytilíni
Variá
Agiássos
968 △ Ólympos
Paleókipos
Loutrá
Agía Marína
Polihnítos
Mesagrós
Pérama
Vrísa
Vaterá
Megalohóri
Skópelos
Paleohóri
Melínda
Plomári
Ágios Isídoros
Híos

Turkey

LESVOS
0   15 km
N

Map
on pages
81 & 82

*A mastic-village house,
Pyrgí, Híos*

(Tues–Sun 8.30am–2.45pm), and superb Roman floor mosaics in the **Archeological Museum annexe** (Tues–Sun 8.30am–2.45pm). Variá, 5km (3 miles) south, has two excellent **art museums**: one devoted to Theofilos Hatzimihaïl, the other a 20th-century collection.

Plomári, Lésvos' second town, is the centre of the ouzo-distilling industry. With your own transport, take the winding road into the hills behind to reach **Agiássos**, 20km (12 miles) inland amid dense pine and chestnut forests. Hot springs erupt at several places – notably Loutrá Géras, Lisvóri, Polyhnítos and Eftalóu, channelled into domed bath-houses. **Mólyvos** in the far north is the most photogenic town, with tiered houses rising to another castle, and its environs are the busiest resort, although 5km (3 miles) south, **Pétra**, with its monolith-church, isn't far behind. From Pétra, head for the Gulf of Kalloní, famous for sardines and the beach at **Skála Kallonís**, or west to the tip of the island at sleepy little **Sígri**.

HIOS

Híos, the purported birthplace of Homer, encompasses pine-clad slopes and fertile citrus groves, sheer limestone cliffs and sandy beaches. It has always been a wealthy place; during Genoese and Ottoman times it was especially prized for its mastic resin, the extruded sap of *Pistacia lentiscus*. This had various uses, including breath-freshening chewing-gum in the sultan's harem. Mastic is still produced today, exclusively in the south of the island, and may have a future as an alternative medicine.

★ **Híos Town** was largely devasted by an 1881 earthquake, but much of the old Genoese citadel and parts of the old quarter survived. Among the score or so of 'mastic villages' in the south, those of ★★ **Mestá**, **Olýmbi** and **Pyrgí** stand out for their maze-like stone architecture and (in the latter case) *xystá*, or embossed surfaces of the houses. The Genoese originally

Agiásmata
Mytilíni
Nagós
Ágio Gála   △1297   Mármaro
Pelinéo   Kardámila
Agía
Markélla
Pityós   Inoússes
Volissós   Lángada
Limniá
Karyés   Vrondádos
Avgónyma
Néa ☩ Híos
Moní
Ág. Geórgios
Sikoúsis   Karfás
Véssa   Thymianá
Liménas
Mestá   Olýmbi   Armólia   TURKEY
Pyrgí   Kómi
Emborió   Sámos
N
HIOS
0   15 km

designed these fortified settlements to protect the mastic-farmers. At the centre of the island, stands the 11th-century ★★**Néa Moní Monastery**, high in a mountain valley. The mosaics in its church (closed for repairs) are among the finest Byzantine artwork of their age. An ossuary chapel near the entrance holds the bones of some of the victims of an 1822 Ottoman massacre. In the same year, the inhabitants of nearby ★**Anávatos** leapt from a summit into a gorge rather than surrender to Turkish forces. Other striking villages dot the countryside, most notably ★**Volissós** in the far northeast, huddled under a crumbled castle.

SAMOS

Still green and fertile even after a series of devastating fires, Sámos is the smallest of the east Aegean isles featured here. Its wine was eulogised by Lord Byron, and the sweet dessert *vin doux* is among the best of its kind. ★**Vathý**, one of the two main ports, is the workaday capital, worth a stop for the superb archeological museum (Tues–Sun 8.30am–3pm), containing finds from the ancient city on the southeast coast, and the adjacent Sanctuary of Hera, of which only one column remains. The old hillside quarter of ★**Áno Vathý** is worth exploring for the dwindling number of Balkan-style houses with overhanging, cantilevered second storeys and pedestrian lanes with runnels down the middle. **Karlóvassi** , the other port, is livelier, thanks to its student population; in between the two lie the coastal resorts of **Ágios Konstandínos** and **Kokkári**. Bus links between Vathý and Karlóvassi are good, but to explore beyond that you'll need a car. The road southwest threads between Ámbelos and Kerketévs – two of the highest summits in the Aegean – to emerge at the sleepy port of **Órmos Marathókambos** and the busy beach of **Votsalákia** just west. Complete a loop of the island by turning east through the foothills to finish at ★**Pythagório**, on the site of ancient Samos, with the harbour still defined by the tyrant Polykrates' jetty.

Star Attractions
- Mestá
- Néa Moní

The Evpalínos Tunnel
This lies above the town of Pythagório and dates from the 6th century BC. For over 1,000 years it helped to supply water to the town from the springs on the far side of Mount Kástro, and in Byzantine times served as a refuge from pirates. Although this example of ancient engineering has collapsed in the middle, it is possible to explore a considerable part of its 1,040-m (3,412-ft) length.

Pythagório harbour

Map below

'Sugar-cube' church, Páros

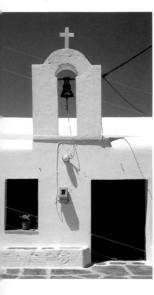

12: The Cyclades

Páros, Náxos, Mýkonos and Santoríni (Thíra) rank among the most beautiful and the most popular of the Cyclades, the archipelago immediately southeast of Attica. Delos (Dílos) lies right at the centre of the Cyclades (meaning 'those around Delos'). In legend the place where Leto gave birth to Apollo, it was a centre of pilgrimage for almost a millennium. Delos was also the hub of political life in the Aegean, through the naval Confederation of Delos, which helped maintain Athenian hegemony over Sparta.

Various seacraft – conventional ferries, high-speed craft and catamarans – serve the Cyclades from Piraeus, Rafína and Lávrio. There are also a few lateral lines between the islands provided by seasonal *kaïkia*. The following sequence has been planned with island-hoppers in mind.

PAROS

★★**Parikía** (pop. 2,000) is the capital and one of the busiest resorts, as well as being the transport hub of the Cyclades. The promenade, with its landmark windmill, is lined with tavernas, ticket agencies and cafeterias; whitewashed

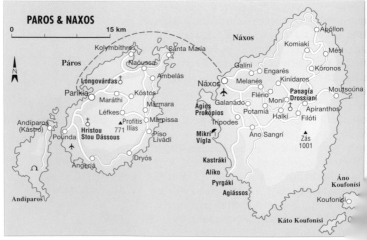

PAROS & NAXOS

0   15 km

N

Náxos

Apóllon
Komiaki
Mési
Kolymbíthres · Santa Maria
Páros
Naóussa
Galíni
Engarés
Kóronos
Ambelás
Melanés
Kinídaros
Moutsoúna
Longovárdas
Náxos
Flério
Panagía Drossianí
Parikía
Kóstos
Agios Prokópios
Galanádo
Moní
Apíranthos
Maráthi
Marmara
Potamiá
Halkí
Filóti
Léfkes
Tripodes
Andíparos (Kástro)
✝ Profítis 771 Ilías
Márpissa
Mikrí Vígla
Áno Sangrí
Zás 1001
Polínda
Hristou Stou Dássous
Píso Livádi
Kastráki
Angeriá
Dryós
Alíko
Áno Koufonísi
Pyrgáki
Agiássos
Andíparos
Koufonísi
Káto Koufonísi

'sugar-cube' houses straggle along the bay and line the main streets. When the Venetians set about building the town in 1260, they made ample use of ancient masonry, which can still be found as integral parts of their fortified *kástro*.

Southeast of the mill, the ★★**Ekatondapylianí** is a rare 6th-century Byzantine church occupying the site of a much older pagan temple. Indeed, much of ancient Paros lies all around, and there's an interesting **archeological museum** documenting the finds. Páros marble, a material that has been highly prized for its translucence since antiquity, was used in the construction of the church. The quarries that supplied the temple-builders over 2,000 years ago lie at the centre of the island, close to the village of Maráthi.

AROUND THE ISLAND

Away from Parikía and the beach resorts, the interior of Páros preserves its tranquil atmosphere. There is a fine view from **Profítis Ilías**, the island's highest peak (770m/2,520ft), which can be climbed from the beautiful village of ★**Léfkes**, where there's a writers' and translators' retreat. The landscape, green or tawny according to season, recedes from the mountain in terraces, and the eye is drawn to the many small white chapels.

★**Náoussa** in the far north is the island's other, trendier holiday resort, set around a pretty harbour where a few fishermen still sit mending nets. At night, waterside tavernas serve their catch, and the port is also the locus of most nightlife; accommodation tends to be pricier and of a better standard than in Parikía. By day, Náoussa's appeal lies in its surrounding beaches and seascapes featuring oddly eroded granite formations; you can walk or take a taxi-boat to a selection of bays, the most famous being **Kolymbíthres**.

NAXOS

The winding alleyways of ★★**Náxos Town**, some arcaded, climb a conical hill. Venetian coats-of-arms adorn houses beneath the medieval fortress.

Star Attractions
● Parikía
● Ekatondapylianí
● Náxos

 Cycladic sculpture
The Bronze-Age Cycladic culture emerged around 3200BC. Perhaps the best known and most impressive artefacts to have been found are the stylised, white marble figurines of women. The pure, simple lines appealed to many 20th-century artists, particularly sculptors, in much the same way that Cycladic architecture struck a chord with architects such as Le Corbusier. The purpose of the figures is unknown, although they are often found in graves, and one of the richest sites is on the uninhabited island of Kéros.

Octopus on display, Náoussa

Map
on page
84 & 86

Visitors in search of the **Archeological Museum** (Tues–Sun 8.30am–3pm) behind the cathedral are likely to lose themselves in the narrow lanes. It's worth the effort to find, as the museum houses an excellent collection of Cycladic figurines from Náxos and various surrounding islands. These mysterious sculptures, created between 2600 and 1600BC, were usually found in graves.

Just northwest of town, on the Palátia peninsula where Theseus abandoned Ariadne, stands ★ **Portára**, the huge entrance portal of an unfinished, 6th-century BC temple to Delian Apollo. There is no more romantic place from which to watch the sunset.

The temple doorway, Náxos

AROUND THE ISLAND

Some of the best beaches in the Cyclades, such as **Ágios Prokópios** and **Agía Ánna**, extend south of Náxos Town. The fertile **Trageá** plain, dominated by silvery-green olive groves, dominates the centre of the island. The village of **Halkí**, with its magnificent medieval tower-houses, is an ideal starting point for a visit to the 6th-century monastery of **Panagía Drossianí**, with frescoes also dating from the 6th century. **Filóti** is the starting point for a path to the top of **Mount Zas** (1,001m/3,280ft), the highest peak in the Cyclades. From the summit there is a view across the plains to the limestone mountains. The road onward from Filóti threads through **Apíranthos**, home village of Manolis Glezos, the resistance hero who tore the swastika-flag down from the Acropolis early in the German occupation.

MYKONOS

★★ **Mýkonos Town** (pop. 4,000) is the quintessential picture-postcard. Brightly coloured fishing boats bob at anchor in the harbour, while dazzlingly white houses aspire to folk-art status. Yachts jostle for space on the quay, as supplies are easily available here. Some wooden-facaded, Venetian-era houses by the sea have been dubbed '**Little Venice**', while the free-form **Paraportianí** chapel must be the most photographed church of hundreds on the island. **Alefkándra** district, inland from Little Venice, is home to art galleries and much of Mykonian **nightlife**. This is (in)famous across Europe, although somewhat less so since the more outrageous transvestite-revue clubs shut down in 2003. Famous too is Petros the pelican, actually the third thus-named bird to have served as this rather over-commercialised town's mascot. At dusk, souvenir shops and fashion outlets overflow with tourists, who later move on to the restaurants and bars.

AROUND THE ISLAND

By day, however, most holidaymakers will be on the south-coast beaches, usually standing-room only, and mostly dominated by various sunbed concessions. Most of the following are accessible by bus or taxi-boat. **Psaroú** beach, with its watersports centre, is now ranked better than overcrowded **Platýs Gialós** next door. Two bays to the east, **Paradise Beach** is busy around the clock, thanks to its campsite-bar, and all-over tans make their appearance. A short walk further east brings you to **Super Paradise** (aka Plindhrí), which gets progressively more gay and nudist as the east end of the beach is approached. **Eliá**,

Star Attractions
● Mýkonos

Gay life
One of the most popular Greek islands, Mýkonos is famed as a resort island for gay men – as Lésvos is, although to a lesser extent, for lesbians. The nightlife is justly famous and is centred on Mýkonos Town – venues are constantly changing so check them out when you arrive. *The* gay beach is Super Paradise, which changes along its length from mixed to overwhelmingly gay and nudist.

Platýs Yialós

Map below

the next cove along, is even longer and nearly as gay; there are more beaches, quieter and more hetero, up to **Kalafátis**, accessible only on foot. Mýkonos is in fact one of the Mediterranean's premier gay resorts, after Ibiza and Sitges in northeast Spain.

Inland, hedges of prickly pear criss-cross a sun-baked, stony landscape; there is only one interior village, **Áno Méra**. Historically, Mýkonos was one of the poorest islands, but tourism has made it one of the wealthiest.

SANTORINI

Santoríni, or **Thíra** to give its official name, is a place that shouldn't be missed. Gaunt coastal cliffs rise dramatically 400m (1,300ft) above sea level, with Firá and Ía villages clinging precariously to the edge. These cliffs are all that remain of a volcano that erupted violently about 3,600 years ago, leaving a submerged caldera in the middle.

Ía's church, perched above the sea

Large ferries arrive at the dull port of Órmos Athiniós, a long bus- or taxi-ride away from the capital of ★★ **Firá**. Largely rebuilt after a devastating earthquake in 1956, the town can't rival Mýkonos for architectural interest but does have a few good museums – and an unrivalled setting. Houses, chapels and (especially) restaurants, linked by steep flights of steps, tumble from the crater's edge; the views, and the sunsets, from the café-terraces over blue church domes and the midnight-blue waters of the abyss, are heart-stopping. Even darker volcanic islets, the result of much later eruptions, poke above the sea; agencies offer day-trips to them.

On ★ **Néa Kaméni**, sulphurous vapours still emanate from an 80-m (260-ft) diameter crater. Just off Paleá Kaméni, visitors bathe in hot springs that burble up at the shore, mixing comfortably with seawater.

In the far north, ★★ **Ía** was also flattened by the quake but more sympathetically reconstructed in white, beige and pink. Once the home of Santoríni's sea captains,

Páros, Náxos

SANTORÍNI

0   5 km

Ía Finikiá
Imerovígli
Thirasía
Manolás   Firá
Néa
Kaméni   Monólithos
Paleá   Karterádos
Kaméni   Mesariá
Athiniós   Éxo Goniá
Áspro   Megalhón Pyrgos Kamári
Profítis † Clássical
Ilías   •Théra
Akrotíri   Périssa
∴ Akrotíri Embório

AEGEAN SEA

it is quieter and more upmarket than Firá, spared the daily stampede of cruise-ship passengers in search of jewellery and furs.

AKROTIRI

Near the island's south tip, at ★★ **Akrotiri** (the name simply means Cape), an ancient site (Tues–Sun 8.30am–3pm) has been uncovered. This flourishing Minoan town was buried by the volcanic eruption of c. 1640BC. Even then, the townspeople lived in two- or three-storey houses which had a rudimentary sewerage system. The walls were decorated with brightly coloured murals, depicting antelopes and children among the most impressive motifs. The carefully restored originals arc in the National Archaeological Museum in Athens *(see page 30)*, although good-quality reproductions are displayed in one of the Firá museums

When archeologist Spyros Marinatos discovered the town, he believed it to be the legendary civilisation of Atlantis, but known contenders for the 'real' Atlantis extend from Cuba to Cyprus. The inhabitants of the ancient town, warned by pre-eruption earthquakes, had sufficient time to escape and take their valuables with them, so unlike at Pompei, no skeletons or vast riches were ever found.

Star Attractions
● **Firá and Ía**
● **Akrotíri**

> **Island hopping**
> Being close together and arranged conveniently in a circle around Delos, the Cyclades are the easiest, and perhaps the most satisfying, of the Greek island chains on which you can 'hop' from one island to the next. There are essentially three ferry routes from Piraeus: the first goes by Ándros, Tínos, Mýkonos and Syros; the second via Páros, Náxos, Íos and Santoríni; and the third through Kýthnos, Sérifos, Sífnos and Mílos.

Firá's spectacular view

Map
on page
91

The Colossus

This enormous statue, one of the Seven Wonders of the Ancient World, was said to have been erected by the local sculptors Kharis and Lakhis in 305BC to celebrate a military victory. The bronze structure depicted Apollo Helios and stood over 30 m (100 ft) high. Legend has it that it straddled the harbour entrance – an impossible feat as it would have had to have been more than 10 times its recorded height. The statue collapsed in an earthquake in 226BC and was finally sold for scrap in the 7th century AD.

Mandráki Harbour

13: Rhodes

When the sun god Helios saw the nymph Rodon under the sea, he induced her to rise to the surface, and married her, giving up his residence on Mount Olympus. Since then, the appeal of Rhodes (Ródos) – biggest of the Dodecanese Islands (pop. 100,000) – has proved irresistible to many others. In Rhodes Town the legacy of the Crusaders is much in evidence; the Knights of St John, under the leadership of their Grand Masters, ruled this island from 1309 to 1522. To protect Rhodes from Ottoman sieges they built 4km (2½ miles) of strong if ultimately futile fortifications.

RHODES OLD TOWN

The 14th century ★★ **Palace of the Grand Masters** (Mon 12.30–8pm, Tues–Sun 8am–8pm), at the old city's highest point, was the inner citadel of the Knights. It was restored by the Italians, who occupied the island from 1912–43. Its upper rooms are paved with Hellenistic mosaics from Kós, while ground-floor galleries concentrate on ancient and medieval Rhodes.

From the palace, the atmospheric ★★ **Street of the Knights** descends east, lined by the facades of medieval inns, once home to the knights and divided by 'tongue' or nationality. The Italians stripped all the Ottman additions from the buildings, revealing coats-of-arms and gargoyles. At the bottom of the gradient, the former Knights' hospital is now the ★ **Archeological Museum** (Tues–Sun 8.30am–3pm); pride of place goes to an exquisite kneeling statue, *Aphrodite Bathing*.

The Ottoman Turkish quarter lay directly south of the palace and hospital, while the Jewish quarter occupied the far eastern side of the walled precinct; after 1522, Christians had to reside outside. Rhodes' many mosques are finally being maintained and repaired. Sokrátous Street, with the reddish-pink Sülemaniye Mosque, was the main commercial street of the town; today commerce is in tourist trinkets. An old, Turkish-run

kafenío with a pebble-mosaic floor contains an astonishing collection of folkloric artefacts. In the Jewish quarter, one suriviving synagogue functions essentially as a memorial to the local community, which vanished in the Nazi death camps.

Star Attractions
● **Palace of the Grand Masters**
● **Street of the Knights**

RHODES NEW TOWN

The Colossus of Rhodes *(see box)* supposedly straddled the entrance to **Mandráki Harbour**. Now, the quay is adorned with a bronze stag and

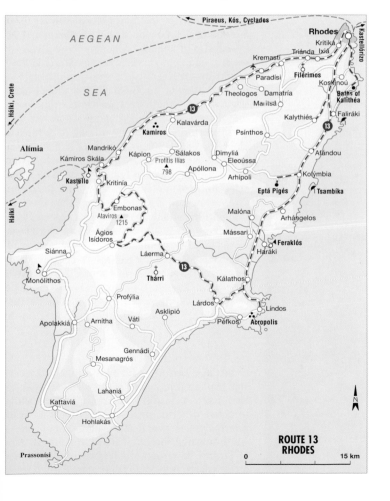

ROUTE 13
RHODES

0   15 km

Map on page 91

Ancient Rhodes
The remnants of ancient Rhodes lie everywhere beneath the medieval city, but are most visible up on the hill of Ágios Stéfanos, where the Hellenistic acropolis includes two evocative columns of an Apollo temple.

doe set on columns. Scattered around the new town are many examples of Internationalist-Rationalist architecture, built by the Italians.

A tour around Rhodes takes about two days. Hiring a car is the only way to make the 200-km (125-mile) trip shown on the map, but you can visit the northwest and southeast coasts separately by bus (station by the Néa Agorá at Mandráki).

THE NORTHWEST COAST

★ **Filérimos hill** (12km/7 miles) is the modern name for the ancient acropolis of Ialysos. The Knights of St John built a monastery here in 1480, on the site of a much older church whose floor mosaic and font survive. Some 3km (2 miles) southwest of Kremastí, a road branches off to the ★★ **Valley of the Butterflies**, a stream-oasis thick with oriental sweetgum trees. In the summer, thousands of visitors come to witness the Jersey tiger moths who gather here. Still further along the coast (30km/20 miles) lies the ancient town of ★★ **Kameiros**, lost amid pines. This, along with Ialysos and Lindos, united late in the 5th century BC to found Rhodes, after which the three went into a gradual decline. None of the foundations of ancient buildings is spectacular, but Kameiros is a uniquely undisturbed Doric townscape. Beyond the modern anchorage of **Kámiros Skála**, with a clutch of fish tavernas, are two of the Knights' rural strongholds: **Kástro Kritinías** (Kastéllo), finely perched with views to Hálki and Alimniá; and the even more dramatically set one near **Monólithos**.

Platía Ippokrátous, Rhodes Old Town

ACROSS THE ISLAND

From there, backtrack through **Siánna**, with roadside stalls selling honey and *soúma* (grappa), to find the road via Ágios Isídoros into the island's forested, deserted interior. A dirt track leads to Láerma, where you detour again 4km (2 miles) south through more forest to the ★ **monastery of Thárri**, home to the most noteworthy frescoes on the island, 14th- and 15th-century masterpieces depicting various miracles. When the road emerges at Lárdos, there are more fine frescoes a short way south at the ★ **church of Asklipió**, in a didactic cartoon-strip style rare in Greece.

THE SOUTHEAST COAST

From Lárdos, head east to the biggest attraction, ★★ **Líndos** (150km/95 miles), a photogenic if commercialised medieval village huddling under its Doric acropolis, enclosed by the walls of yet another Knights' castle. The Athena temple and Hellenistic stoa will be scaffolded for years to come, but the views along the coast are superb. Líndos has two beaches: a northerly one with amenities, and the southerly, well-protected, less crowded St Paul's Bay.

The village of **Arhángelos** lies between the beaches of **Agía Agáthi** and **Tsambíka**. On the crag above the latter is **Tsambíka monastery**, a pilgrimage place for childless women on 8 September; the church is festooned with photos of babies born through the Virgin's intervention.

Just past Tsambíka, turn inland to visit the oasis of ★ **Eptá Pigés**, where a tunnel links the 'seven springs' with a woodland pond. Last stop is ★ **Thérmes Kallithéas**, an Italian spa complex in orientalised Art Deco style that's been the location for numerous film and advertising shots.

Star Attractions
● **Valley of the Butterflies**
● **Kameiros**
● **Lindos**

Below: Líndos housing
Bottom: looking out from Tsambíka Monastery

*The Lion Fountain,
Platía Venizélou*

14: Crete

The islanders of Crete (Kríti) have retained their customs, cuisine and traditional music traditions more than people anywhere else in the country. The shepherds bind a tassled black cloth around their heads, pull on leather, calf-high boots and call themselves Cretan first, Greek second.

IRÁKLIO

★ **Iráklio** (pop. 150,000) is the first place most visitors encounter. The best view of the old town, now rather dwarfed by concrete sprawl, is from the Venetian harbour and walls of the ★ **Venetian fortifications**. Odós 25-Avgoústou leads to ★ **Platía Venizélou**, named after the statesman, who was a Cretan. Venetian governor-general Francesco Morosini had the **Lion Fountain** built at the centre in 1628; the surrounding cafés serve *bougátsa* – a pastry filled with sweet or savoury cheese. Round the corner in ★ **Odós 1866** is the town's central bazaar, overflowing with stalls sell-

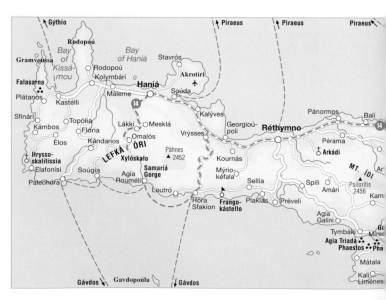

ing anything from cheap souvenirs to delicious Cretan yoghurt in clay pots to local saffron. The market ends by the Venetian **Bembo Fountain** – the Turkish pump-house just beyond functions as a tiny *kafenío*.

The ★★★ **Archeological Museum** (Apr–Sept: Mon 12–7pm, Tues–Sun 8am–7pm; Oct–Mar: daily 8am–5pm) on Platía Eleftherías houses finds from the era of the first Cretan settlers, the Minoans. For many visitors it is the main reason to visit Iráklio. The Phaestos disc, a clay tablet with 241 undeciphered characters, a drinking rhyton in the shape of a bull's head, and the faience snake goddess are some of the most prized exhibits. Beautiful jewellery includes a delicate pair of earrings in the shape of bees. Displayed upstairs are the famous frescoes from palaces across the island, but particularly Knossós.

KNOSSOS

Archeologists consider ★★★ **Knossos** (5km/3 miles, Knossós in modern Greek) to be a religious and commercial centre as well as a royal palace,

Star Attractions
● **Archaeological Museum**
● **Knossos**

Kazantzákis' tomb
The great Cretan writer Nikos Kazantzákis is buried in the Martinengo Bastion on Iráklio's Venetian walls. These were built in the 15th century, and in some places are 29m(95ft) thick, making Iráklio one of the most formidable fortresses in the Mediterranean in its day. From the grave site there is a view of the mountains surrounding the city.

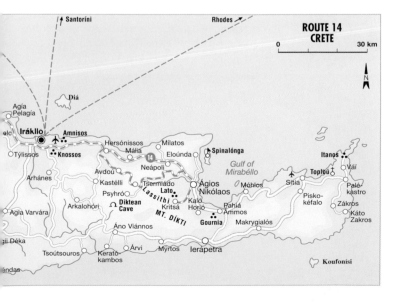

Map on pages 94–5

Below: Knossos
Bottom: Mátala beach from inside one of the caves

and a visit will give an insight into Minoan life and culture. Sir Arthur Evans took 40 years to uncover and reconstruct the vanished palace, which existed almost four millennia earlier. The site (Apr–Sept: daily 8am–7pm; Oct–Mar: 8.30am–3pm) is more than the usual bare foundations and heaps of stones. The Throne Room contains a well-used stone throne, and there are clay urns in the storerooms – their design has been scarcely modified in modern versions. The queen's chambers, with their blue dolphin fresco (a copy; the original is in the Iráklio museum) are essential viewing.

WEST FROM IRAKLIO

Crete lends itself to separate tours, and there is a decent bus service on which to make them. In Iráklio, buses east and west along the coast, and to Knossos, leave from the station at the harbour; buses to Phaestos, Mátala with its beach caves, and Agía Galíni leave from another terminal at the Hánia Gate.

As you head west along the coast, a road branches off the main highway towards **Fódele** (30km/20 miles), nestled amid citrus groves. A signposted path leads to the supposed birthplace of the painter Domenikos Theotokopoulos, who is better known as El Greco.

RETHYMNO AND AROUND

★★★ **Réthymno** (pop. 30,000) has not been spoilt by the touristic development behind the 10-km (6-mile) sandy beach just east. The old town, a jumble of Venetian and Ottoman buildings along narrow lanes, crowds the old fishing harbour with its expensive but romantically set tavernas. Town and harbour huddle beneath a huge **Venetian fortress** (Sat–Thur 8.30am–7pm), built to protect Réthymno after repeated pirate raids. Near the Nerantzís mosque with its minaret, a worthwhile ★ **Folklore Museum** (Mon–Sat 9am–2pm, 6–8pm) is housed in a Venetian mansion.

RURAL MONASTERIES

Sited in the Psilorítis foothills southeast of Réthymno, ★ **Arkádi Monastery** is a shrine to the long struggle to liberate Crete from Ottoman rule. In 1866, when the monastery faced annihilation, the abbot ordered the powder magazine to be blown up. Hundreds of rebels and civilians taking refuge in the monastery died as a result, along with many attackers, and the skulls of some victims are kept on display.

Due south of Réthymno , looking over terraces to the the Libyan Sea, ★ **Préveli Monastery** (Apr–May: daily 8am–7pm; Jun–Oct: Mon–Sat 8am–1.30pm, 3.30–8pm, Sun 8am–8pm) was another centre of resistance during the Ottoman occupation. The local rebellious spirit was put to good effect during World War II, when the monks helped evacuate Allied troops after the Battle of Crete. The evacuation to Egypt took place from nearby ★ **Palm Beach**, so named for the date palms that grow just inland along the Kourtaliótiko River. Once idyllic, the sandy beach suffers chronic litter problems from rough campers and day-trippers.

HANIA

★★ **Haniá** (pop. 70,000; 150km/93 miles), the island's capital until 1971, is Crete's proudest town. The modern quarters are featureless if pleasant, but the Venetian-Turkish old town is a

Star Attractions
● Réthymno
● Haniá

Psilorítis
The highest point on Crete is Mount Psilorítis, or Ída, at 2,456m (8,056ft). It is a relatively easy ascent from Anógia via the Nída Plateau. At the summit, Tímios Stavrós, is a chapel from where the views are superb. On the way up you pass the Ída cave, a contender for the birthplace of Zeus, sealed off for an archaeological dig. The Nida plateau still sees transhumance, when the shepherds bring their flocks up in summer to graze, and make cheese from the sheep's milk.

Elafonísi, far western Crete

Map on pages 94–5

Map on pages 94–5

Sfakiá

This region in southwestern Crete is famed for its independent and fierce population – blood feuds were common here until relatively recently. The Sfakiots were valiant in their resistence to Turkish and German occupiers, and helped Allied forces escape after the German invasion of 1941. The main town of Sfakiá is Hóra Sfakíon, from where you can get a boat to Gávdos, Europe's southernmost point.

Haniá harbour at dusk

gem, rivalled only by Réthymno's. There are two old harbours: the main one, with the 17th-century Mosque of the Janissaries, and the smaller, 'inner' one, flanked by Venetian *arsenália* or boat-houses and overlooked by Kastélli hill, focus of the Minoan, Byzantine and Venetian city. The French-style market hall is one of Greece's finest, its stalls full of fish, fresh produce, cheese, olive oil, herbs and honey.

THE GORGE OF SAMARIA

Every morning between May and October, buses run from Haniá to Crete's most impressive natural phenomenon, the ★★★ **Gorge of Samariá**, 42km (26 miles) to the south. A walk through the 18-km (11-mile) long gorge, one of the most dramatic in Europe, begins beyond the Omalós plain at Xylóskalo. Initially one descends steeply through forest, with the **Lefká Óri** (White Mountains) all around; soon walkers are in the rocky stream bed, a raging torrent in winter when the gorge is off-limits. About halfway along stands abandoned Samariá village, whose inhabitants were forced to leave when the area was declared a nature reserve in 1965.

At one point – the Sidéresportes – the gorge measures only 3.5m (11ft) wide, with 500-m (1,640-ft) vertical cliffs towering above. After a six-hour walk the southern Mediterranean and the hamlet of Agía Rouméli, with its cluster of expensive tavernas, is reached. Boats ferry passengers from here to Hóra Sfakíon, where buses for Haniá are waiting.

Alternatively, it's possible to take a boat west to the resorts of Soúgia and Paleohóra, from where you can visit the island of ★ **Elafonísi**, with a beach and a warm, shallow lagoon.

LASSITHI

The second tour heads east from Iráklio, climbing initially to the ★★ **Lassíthi Plateau** (35km/21 miles). The top of the pass is the best place to appreciate the circular plain, with its vegetable patches and orchards. As many as 10,000 cloth-sailed windmills once irrigated the high plain, but except for a handful that operate only in late spring, they have been superseded by electrical pumps. There are claims that the ★ **Diktean cave** at the southern edge of the plateau – like the Idean cave on Psilorítis – is the birthplace of Zeus.

AGIOS NIKOLAOS AND KRITSA

★ **Ágios Nikólaos** (pop. 8,000; 70km/43 miles), overlooking the Bay of Mirabéllo, is the St Tropez of Crete – although there is no beach to speak of. The restaurants and bars lining the harbour, and the supposedly bottomless saltwater lake (actually about 60m/195ft deep) in the town centre, are the places to see and be seen. Nightlife in Ágios Nikólaos continues well into the early hours of the morning, with most of the clubs along 25-Martíou or the harbourside.

★ **Kritsá**, 10km (6 miles) inland, is a quieter and less expensive place to stay, and is famous for its handicrafts. Níkos Kazantzákis' novel *The Greek Passion* was filmed here, in what was then an unspoiled mountain village. Some 2km (1 mile) below Kritsá stands the white church of ★★ **Panagía Kyrá** (Mon–Sat 9am–3pm, Sun 9am–2pm), which contains some of the best late-Byzantine frescoes on Crete.

Star Attractions
- **Samariá Gorge**
- **Lassíthi**
- **Panagía Kyrá**

Below: Lassíthi windmills
Bottom: Samariá
vantage point

Map
below

A writer on Corfu
Lawrence Durrell is just one of many literary figures to have found contentment on Corfu. Its bays and woods inspired his chronicle of the 1930s, *Prospero's Cell*.

15: Corfu

Strikingly green and Italian-influenced, Corfu (Kérkya) is the second largest of the Ionian islands. It has enchanted foreigners for centuries, from William Shakespeare who used it, thinly veiled, as the setting for *The Tempest*, to Henry Miller and Lawrence Durrell in the 1930s. Italian dishes are prominent on menus, and Italians themselves turn out in large numbers come summer, along with Greeks and northern Europeans. Sandy beaches, aquamarine sea, olive groves and old fortresses combine to create an island that is still magical despite patches of overdevelopment. The road network is extensive – if often narrow and

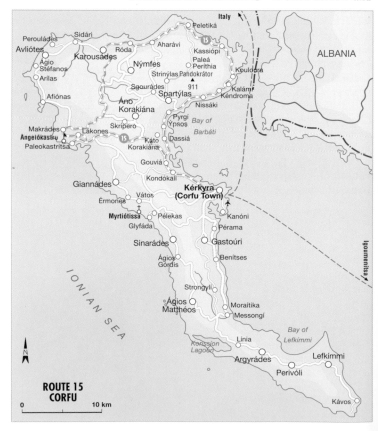

ROUTE 15
CORFU

0   10 km

dangerous – so any point on Corfu can be reached by car or bus in a day.

The Venetian occupiers had their headquarters at ★★★ **Corfu (Kérkyra) Town** (pop. 30,000) from 1386–1797. They improved the existing Byzantine ★ **Paleó Froúrio**, and built the ★ **Néo Froúrio**: fortresses that offer unrivalled views over tiled roofs. When Napoleon annexed the Ionian Islands in 1797, he brought French refinement in the form of the ★★ **Spianáda**, supposedly modelled on the rue de Rivoli in Paris. Fancy cafés shelter under the arcades of the tall buildings flanking the Spianáda on the west, while a cricket ground laid out by the English in the park adds to the sophistication of this elegant town. In 1815 the Napoleonic Empire was distributed by the Congress of Vienna, with the Ionian Islands falling under British administration until 1864 and union with Greece. Yet the Venetian atmosphere remains: behind the commercial streets are narrow alleys, with painted shutters, iron balconies and washing hanging out to dry.

AROUND THE ISLAND

Beyond Pýrgi, the coast is less densely populated as the road becomes a spectacular corniche. More exclusive resorts like ★ **Kouloúra** and ★ **Kalámi** huddle at the toes of ★ **Mount Pandokrátor** (906m/2,971ft), the highest mountain on Corfu. All along this 'Corfiot Rivera', up to the port-resort of ★ **Kassiópi** (35km/22 miles), Albania sprawls just across narrow straits. Beyond Kassiópi, the road straightens and the shore gets sandier as you pass heavy development before turning south. It's easy to detour slightly from the map to quieter beaches below **Perouládes** and **Afiónas** before arriving at Byzantine-Venetian ★★ **Angelókastro**, 300m (1,000ft) above the sea, with sweeping views over the northwest coast and the Diapóndia islets. From Lakónes you look down on three bays framed by fissured rocks: ★ **Paleokastrítsa** (70km/45 miles). The beaches are lovely, with the added attraction of scuba-diving, but hopelessly crowded in summer.

Star Attraction
● Corfu Town
● Spianáda

Below: a Spianáda arcade
Bottom: Angelokástro

Greek Art History

MINOAN-MYCENAEAN

The palaces at Knossos *(see page 95)* and Phaestos date from the Minoan-Mycenaean civilisation (2600–1100BC). The frescoes at the Iráklio, Athens and Santoríni archeological museums suggest a peaceable, refined culture with a high appreciation of luxury, but recent excavations at Anemospiliá on Crete suggest that in exceptional circumstances – particularly the earthquakes and tidal waves arising from the volcanic collapse of Thera – human sacrifice was resorted to. Minoan artefacts illuminate aspects of life at the royal court: women were using a form of lipstick, drinking from painted cups and wearing ornate jewellery. After the final collapse of the Minoan dynasty, aesthetic features of the culture reached the Peloponnese, where the builders of Mycenae and Tiryns employed Cretan artisans to decorate the interiors of their citadels.

The Dorians
Over the course of the 11th and 10th centuries BC, Crete and Mycenae were destroyed and their culture vanished. Their successors, the Dorians (who included the 'Sea Peoples' from the east), favoured a more austere style. They decorated household objects and vases with geometric patterns, triangles and the ancient Indian swastika. The superb collection in the Athens National Archaeological Museum *(see page 30)* documents the progression of ancient art, while the collections in Iráklio museum contain the most important finds from Minoan sites.

ARCHAIC

Between 700 and 500BC the Dorians, Ionians and Aeolians introduced Egyptian and Middle Eastern styles into art, particularly in sculpture. Statues from this era display the same formal bearing as Egyptian finds from the same period. But this rigidity disappears in the course of the 6th century BC, and artists softened the faces of their subjects with what is known as the 'Archaic smile'.

Architecture, particularly the relief frieze, was influenced by the literature of the poets who told tales of gods and heroes, beginning with the Homeric epics, which were common currency by the 8th century BC. The stonemasons who toiled away at the 6th-century BC temples were conversant with such tales, and legends surrounding the Olympian deities, as the scenes that adorn the pediments often depict their heroic deeds.

New forms also emerged in Archaic vase painting. From the 6th century BC onwards, black figures embellish red-clay vases, which adorned the living rooms of wealthier Greeks, with the artists

Opposite: Hermes by Praxiteles
Below: fresco from Knossos

preferring scenes from everyday life rather than abstract motifs. Legends are also depicted, such as the scene of Achilles and Ajax involved in a board game. Over time, black figures give way to red and, on vases with a black background, the figures were embossed. Vase illustrations provide much valuable information about everyday life – two of the best collections are found in the National Museum and Museum of Cycladic and Ancient Greek Art in Athens *(see pages 30–31).*

Below: Archaic vase painting
Bottom: a Roman frieze

CLASSICAL

Everyday life between 500 and 336BC, a period of outstanding artistic and intellectual creativity, was shadowed by war and plague, although one group to benefit were the sculptors of gravestone reliefs or steles, erected by families in honour of their dead.

Artistic standards for centuries to come were set during the Classical years, with Phidias outstanding among sculptors. Idealised gods and human figures were depicted with muscular, anatomically correct bodies and noble faces. He fashioned the statue of Zeus at Olympia *(see page 53)* from gold and ivory as well as the goddess Athena on the Acropolis in Athens *(see page 27).* These sculptures, as well as the Parthenon friezes, were painted in bright colours.

ROMAN

From 146BC until the 4th century AD, Greek art was largely subsumed into Roman culture. When the Romans conquered Greece, they were profoundly influenced by its artistic ethos. The works they created in late Hellenistic style were so convincingly that for many years examples were assumed to be from the workshops of earlier, Greek artists. A good example is the Laocoön group sculpture displayed in Rome's Vatican Museum; this depicts an incident from the Trojan War, in which Poseidon sends a sea-serpent to devour the Trojan high priest Laocoön, who had warned against accepting the Wooden Horse. In the major cities of the expanding Roman empire, sculptors simply copied Greek originals in order to meet the demand for subjects that had found favour among wealthy Romans.

In the realm of architecture, however, the Romans were highly original, combining traditional Greek styles with their own rounded arch and vaulting designs, and extensive use of brick. The Emperor Hadrian (AD117–38), wanting to make his own mark on Athens, commissioned several buildings in the city, including Hadrian's Library *(see page 29)*.

> **Hellenistic Art**
> Splendid colours were retained during the Hellenistic period (336–146BC). Architects designed market halls and baths, living quarters and private houses. The reconstructed buildings in the Agora in Athens demonstrate the achievements of the Hellenistic architects *(see page 23)*.
>
> Sculptors took the Classical style a step further. Instead of remote gods and perfect human forms, they now carved more natural statues out of large marble blocks. Heroes were shown at times of defeat as well – it was no longer fashionable to show the hero outshining all others. Artists also chose to work with less solemn themes. One celebrated example of Hellenistic sculpture is on display in the Athens National Archaeological Museum: in the piece known as *Aphrodite, Eros and Pan,* a seduction scene is portrayed in stone.

BYZANTINE

During the 4th century AD the Roman Empire was divided into Eastern and Western sections, with Byzantium (later Constantinople) as capital of the Eastern Roman, or Byzantine, Empire. The Western empire soon collapsed, but the predominantly Greek-speaking, Orthodox Eastern half endured as a political and cultural power for nearly a millennium. Church architecture began as a modification of the basilica, the favourite building-form of the Romans, but later evolved into more complicated structures, particularly the cross-in-square floor plan crowned with several domes. As central cupolas became higher and weightier, ingenious methods of supporting them – sometimes without columns – were devised. This style still characterises Greek churches.

Byzantine Virgin and Child, Thessaloníki

Byzantine mosaic

Sculpture was neglected in favour of frescoes and mosaics; some fine examples of these art forms can be seen in the churches of Mystrás, Kastoriá and Thessaloníki *(see pages 49, 67 and 71)*.
Frescoes went through several phases of evolution, including Renaissance-influenced 'post-Byzantine' styles, executed after the fall of Constantinople in 1453, and the marked differences allow accurate dating of images. Many early paintings were destroyed in the 8th century during the austere Iconoclastic controversy. Mosaics, a far more expensive medium, were not made after the 11th century; skilful use of the *tesserae* (tiny, pigmented component stones), often against a golden background, give the best ones a remarkable fluidity and three-dimensionality. Icons or images of the Orthodox saints were also given a golden background, and the attributes of each saint were codified early on, with modern icon-painters still rigidly adhering to them.

MUSIC AND CINEMA

Greece has a range of traditional music *(dimotikí mousikí)*. It has been in decline since the 1960s and the advent of electrical amplification, but a generation of young musicians is attempting to recapture the skill and ethos. Moreover, excellent archival recordings are available. The music of the smaller Aegean islands *(nisiótika)* differs noticeably from that of the mainland and Crete.

Cretan music is dominated by the *lýra*, a three-stringed lap fiddle used to accompany dance and song. The *lýra* is often accompanied by the *laoúto*, related to the mandolin and now only used as rhythm backing. Classic recordings feature the late Kostas Moundakis and Nikos Xylouris; contemporary performers include Psarandonis and the group Haïnides. *Nisiótika* from the Cyclades and Dodecanese traditionally relied on violin and *sandoúri* (hammer dulcimer), although the former is now amplified and the latter replaced by a rock-style rhythm section. Among better recordings are those by Nikos Ikonomidis, Emilia Hatzidaki, and sisters Anna Karabessini and Efi Sarri.

Venetian influences

At the beginning of the 13th century the Venetians, under the flag of the Lion of St Mark, seized sections of the coastal mainland and some of the islands. Venetian and Byzantine architecture came to influence each other, with the cathedral of San Marco in Venice consequently displaying many Byzantine features. The Venetians, on the other hand, left behind in Greece a number of magnificent examples of their architecture. Towns such as Náfplio *(see page 41)*, Iráklio and Réthymno *(see pages 94 and 97)* are dominated by extensive fortresses, and Greek fishermen unload their catches in the Venetian harbours. The Venetians built the fortifications in order to protect themselves in their struggle against the Ottoman Turks.

On the mainland, traditional music is dominated by the clarinet, although here too the guitar, violin and lap-drum accompaniment has been replaced by electric keyboards, etc. Contemporary recordings of Petro-Loukas Halkias, Yiorgos Koros and folk revivalist Domna Samiou offer a more acoustic sound. Macedonia and Thrace have produced excellent folk vocalists such as Xanthippi Karathanasi and Kronis Aïdonidis.

REBETIKA

Often billed flippantly as 'the Greek blues', *rebétika* was the music of the social margins in Athens, Piraeus and Thessaloníki. Although *rebétika* had existed in some form since well before the turn of the 20th century, it was only after 1922, when over a million Greek refuges arrived from Asia Minor, that modern *rebétika* emerged. Early songs, often extolling the pleasures of hash-smoking and the woes of illness, jail and hopeless love, were played on *bouzoúki*, guitar and *baglamás*, and at first restricted to the *tekédes* (hash dens). By the late 1930s and 1940s, the music had acquired a broader appeal, and more 'overground' venues. By the 1950s, further changes in taste and orchestration (especially in the tuning of the *bouzoúki*) made this music mainstream, and true *rebétika* ceased to exist.

Rebétika musicians in Piraeus

Singer-songwriters

Éntekno and *laikí* paved the way for the emergence of a generation of singer-songwriters. They drew on an eclectic range of influences from Bob Dylan, to rock music, to Greek gypsy dances. Names to look out for include Dionysus Savvopoulos, Nikos Xydakis, Nikos Papazoglou and Nikos Portokaloglou.

Luckily, recordings of its golden age abound; the most important early performers include Rosa Eskenazi, Rita Abatzi and Andonis Dalgas, while Ioannis Papaïoannou and the Piraeus Quartet with Markso Vamvakaris dominated the 1930s. After World War II, Vassilis Tsitsanis had uncontested sway, with vocalists including Ioanna Yiorgapopoulou, Sotiria Bellou and Marika Ninou.

Entekhno and Laiki

Rebétika inspired two other styles, *éntekhno* and *laïkí*, both emerging in the 1950s. The former first emerged in the symphonic compositions of Mikis Theodorakis and Manos Hatzidakis, with Stavros Xarhakos and Ioannis Markopoulos appearing in the 1960s. They incorporated traditional instruments and melodies into rich orchestral textures. Theodorakis' songs provided a focus for clandestine dissent during the junta years. *Laïkí* music was closer to *rebétika* in spirit and instrumentation, with gypsy and/or Anatolian rhythms thrown in. Stars of this genre include Stelios Kazantzidis and the prolific Yiorgos Dalaras.

Film

A number of Greek producers have made names for themselves. Michael Cacoyannis, a Hollywood producer of Cypriot origin, made *Zorba the Greek* in 1964, based on the novel by Nikos Kazantzakis, with Anthony Quinn as Zorba.

Anthony Quinn as Zorba

Costas Costa-Gavras's 1969 film Z dealt with the assassination of leftist deputy Grigoris Lambrakis by thugs working with the connivance of the 1963 regime, and the murder's subsequent cover-up, which brought down the Karamanlis government. In this and later films, Costa-Gavras worked with international stars, something that Theo Angelopoulos rarely does, emphasising instead elegiac camera-work and minimal dialogue. His reputation was established with his marathon *Thiasos (The Travelling Players)*, while *Alexander the Great* received the Golden Lion at the 1980 Venice Film festival. A mixed output since has included *The Beekeeper*, *Landscape in the Mist*, *Journey to Kythira* and *Ulysses' Gaze*.

FESTIVALS AND HOLIDAYS

Between May and October artistic events often take place outdoors. The Hellenic Festival, staged in Athens and Epidaurus, is the best known, but every sizeable town has a programme of open-air concerts, usually on the harbour quay or sports stadium. The only firm information for these local happenings is fly-posters and leaflets in the nearest tourist office.

1 January: Feast of St Vassilios (Basil); adults play cards for money; a cake (the *vassilópita*) with a lucky coin inside is baked.

6 January: Epiphany *(Theofánia)*; the local priest blesses the closest body of water, and throws in a cross, to be retrieved by young men.

Carnival: Seven weeks before Easter (pre-Lent), Carnival or *Apókreas* is celebrated with mummery and parties.

25 March: Annunciation *(Evangelismós)*, observed most fervently on Tínos; also marks the start of the 1821 revolt against Turkish rule.

Easter: The major Greek Orthodox festival *(see page 11).*

1 May: Labour Day *(Protomagiá)*; balconies and front doors are festooned with wreaths.

21 May: The *Anastenaría* at Langadás near Thessaloníki. Fire-dancers, in a partial trance and holding icons, shuffle across hot coals.

15 August: Feast of the Assumption *(Kímisis tis Panagías)*. The country closes down for a few days, and *panigíria* (musical festivals) erupt in any village with a church dedicated to the Virgin's 'Falling Asleep'.

28 October: 'Óhi Day' celebrates the apocryphal one-word answer Greek dictator Metaxás gave to Mussolini's ultimatum of 1940, demanding 'free passage' for his forces (*óhi* means no).

25 December: Christmas *(Hristoúgena)*; not nearly as important, or as commercialised, as in Western Europe and the US.

Below: many festivals are religious
Bottom: packed Odeon of Herodes Atticus for the Athens Festival

FOOD AND DRINK

Greek cuisine, like its music, draws on influences from the Middle East and Italy, with a small kernel remaining of traditional late-Roman and Byzantine fare – in which tomatoes, potatoes and citrus fruits were unknown. The grilled-meat-and-chips platters and (worse) fast-food stalls of the typical resort or city centre are the worst representation imaginable for a Mediterranean diet that has been centuries in the making.

Eating outside at a small wooden table in a narrow alley, by a harbour or behind a beach is a quintessential part of a Greek summer meal. Menus exist, but they are more to reassure you about the price range of the restaurant than to indicate what is actually available; usually, only dishes with a price next to them are on offer. Greeks typically choose from the waiter's recitation of the day's special dishes; foreigners may still be ushered over to the steam-tray battery to choose pre-prepared dishes, thus circumventing the language barrier. Such dishes are served lukewarm; Greeks believe that piping-hot food is actually bad for you.

The main eateries style themselves as *tavérnes*, *estiatória* or even *inomagiría*; differences are hard to spot, although the latter two categories are more likely to produce such substantial, stereotypical dishes as *moussakás* (mincemeat and slices of aubergine and potatoes coated in béchamel), *yiouvétsi* (pasta and meat chunks in a clay dish) and *pastítsio* (macaroni pie).

Psarotavérnes specialise in fish. Here you choose your fish from those on display and pay according to uncleaned weight, but as everywhere in the Med, fish is no longer cheap,

Opposite: fresh fruit and vegetables in Argostóli market

and farmed items abound – best stick to the humbler, seasonal fare such as *atherína* (sand smelt), *gávros* (anchovies) and *sardélles* (sardines). A *psistaría* emphasises grilled meat and salad, while an *ouzerí* or *mezedopolío* offers a variety of *mezedákia* or little platters of delicacies such as *taramosaláta*, *tyropitákia* (small cheese pies), *fáva* (broad bean) purée, sausages, marinated seafood titbits and *saganáki* (fried cheese), all presented on a large tray or *dískos* for you to choose, followed by hot dishes by individual order.

DRINK

To wash this all down, there's a vast selection of wine, among which the better labels are finally getting the recognition they deserve after years where *retsína* – white wine flavoured with pine resin, the oenological equivalent of Zorba's Dance – has closed minds to the possibility of anything else worth drinking. Mass-market brands such as Boutari, Cambas or Tsantali appear on most lists, but better vintners worth looking for include Papaïoannou, Lazarides, Tselepou and Carras. Inexpensive barrelled wines (*hýma* or *me to kiló*) served in flagons *(kandária)* are making a comeback after almost disappearing in the early 1990s. The quality is pot-luck – it's always best to start with a quarter- or half-litre – but when they're good they can match bottled varieties. Several brands of lager (including the country's first micro-brewery, Craft) are available (served very chilled), and imported German, British, French and Belgian brews are usually offered at the better bars.

Distilled grape spirits are popular, and produced locally in several versions of varying strength: *oúzo* on

Sámos, Híos, Mytilíni and Týrnavo in Thessaly, *soúma* on Sámos and Rhodes, *tsípouro* across the northern mainland, *tsikoudiá* or *rakí* on Crete. These all are based on the mash left over after the must has been extracted, and variably flavoured (or not) with different botanical essences: anise for *oúzo*, pear or cinnamon (or nothing) for *tsípouro*, nothing for *rakí*. Brandy means Metaxas, available in three-, five- or seven-star strength.

HOME COOKING AND COFFEE

Food plays a pivotal role in everyday family life. Amid endless discussions of where it was bought and how it was prepared, families sit at table enjoying a leisurely meal – typically 3– 4.30pm for lunch. Even basic commodities such as bread and olive oil arouse strong opinions, and the humble tomato is greatly admired. Specimens may be passed around among connoisseurs who extol its virtues. Home cooking is, except during the warmer

---

The *kafenío*

The *kafenío* is less a café, more a social institution – a meeting-place for the menfolk and, in the remoter villages, functions as an office, bank, post office and political headquarters. It is here that business is conducted, lawyers are consulted, credit arranged, politics and football discussed and the latest fashions worn by the tourists admired. Women are not welcome in this male bastion. Drinking is only of secondary importance, although an occasional *oúzo* may be consumed. Some may play cards or *távli* (backgammon), others may sit in silence watching the world go by. No man will enter the *kafenío* without his *kombolói* – a small chain of stone or wooden beads. Carried to relieve tension or anxiety, the *kombolói* is like a rosary or the 'worry beads' used by men in Islamic countries, but it has no religious significance.

---

months when *mangália* (barbecues) make their appearance on pavements and verandahs, likely to centre on the more involved *magireftá* (casserole dishes) such as *briám* (ratatouille) and fancy sweets based on *fyllo* dough. These obviously take up much of a housewife's time, and in the old days a measure of her virtue was her skill at, and dedication to, such recipes, in contrast to quickly prepared fried or grilled items, which were dismissed as *to faï tis poutánas* (whore's food).

Coffee remains a popular end to a meal at home. The traditional Greek coffee (really the same formula from Yemen to Bulgaria) is made in a small, long-handled vessel, the *bríki*, from arabica beans ground super-fine and gently 'bumped' in boiling water to produce a froth or *kaïmáki*. This is served, together with the grounds, in small cups, in a choice of three ways: *skéto* (unsweetened), *métrio* (a spoonful of sugar), or *glykó* (cloyingly sweet). Certain elderly women specialise in telling fortunes from the patterns left by the sediment in the cups. Instant coffee, known generically as *nes(kafé)* after that ubiquitous brand, is also common, although better varieties are now appearing as filter-grade, and every café now aspires to offer either *fíltro kafé* or even (with varying degrees of authenticity) cappuccinos and espressos. A glass of water is always served with coffee.

These suggested restaurants are listed in the following price categories: €€€ = expensive, €€ = moderate, € = inexpensive

Athens

Baïraktaris, Platía Monastiráki 2; tel: 210 321 3036. One of Athens' oldest restaurants; serves cheap, wholesome food – *fasoláda* (bean soup), *domátes gemistés* (stuffed tomatoes) and *fáva*. €
Dimokratous, Dimokrítou 23, Kolonáki;

tel: 210 361 3588. In a neoclassical mansion; good, standard Greek food – salads, *fáva*, *hórta*, grilled meat. The house wine is palatable and prices reasonable. €€

Frame, Kleoménous 2, Kolonáki; tel: 210 7290 711. Trendy new restaurant in the refurbished St George Lycabettus Hotel. The food is Mediterranean (lots of tomatoes, olive oil, grilled meat and fish), and of a high standard. €€

Kioupi, Platía Kolonáki 4; tel: 210 361 4033. A cheap, friendly and spotless cellar restaurant. There is usually a fine selection of *bámies* (green beans stewed in oil), *hórta* and chicken dishes. €

Platanos, Diogénous 4, Pláka; tel: 210 322 0666. A taverna close to the Roman Agora. Not that cheap, but serves good, basic food, including vegetable dishes, as well as grilled and baked meats. €€

Thanasis, Mitropóleous 69, Monastiráki; tel: 210 324 4705. This Athenian institution is the place to eat *souvláki*, best washed down with chilled beer. €

Vasilenas, Etolikoú 72, Piraeus; tel: 210 461 2457. Justly famous for its huge list of *mezédes*, this plain-looking taverna is open evenings only. Very popular, so booking is essential. €€

Corfu

La Famiglia, Maniarízi and Arlióti 30, Kérkyra Town; tel: 266 103 0270. Greek/Italian-run bistro specialising in salads and pasta. Excellent value and efficient service; reservations essential. Open evenings only. €€

Mouragia, Arseníou 15, Kérkyra Town; tel: 266 103 3815. A good mix of seafood and Corfiot *magirevtá* such as *sofríto* and *pastitsáda*. Inexpensive, and great sea views into the bargain. €

Crete

Ionia, corner Évans/Giánnari, tel: 281 028 3213, Iráklio. Has been offering good Greek meat, fish and vegetable dishes since 1923. €€

Ippokambos, Mitsotáki 2, Iráklio; tel:

281 028 0240. A superb establishment overlooking the old harbour, famed for its meticulously prepared *mezédes*. Usually packed with locals, so go early. €€

Kyriakos, Dimokratías 51, Iráklio; tel. 281 022 2464. Traditionally cooked Cretan meat, fish and vegetable dishes. €€

Anaplous, Sífaka 34, Maherádika, Haniá; tel: 282 104 1320. Modishly set in a restored ruin; traditional Cretan dishes including pork baked in a clay pot. €€

Karnagio, Platía Kateháki 8, Haniá; tel: 282 105 3366. Set back from the harbour, in an old *hamám* (steam bath). Beloved by local people, it serves quality Cretan and vegetarian dishes. €€

Kastoriá

Doltso, Tsakáli 2; tel: 246 702 4670. Opened in 2003, this classy place on Doltso Square has become one of the local favourites. The restored mansion in which it's housed is all stone and wood. The top-class food includes many traditional Macedonian dishes. €€€

Mýkonos

Matthew Taverna, Tourlós (on the Ág. Stéfanos road; no phone). This is a polished taverna; service on the cool terrace is friendly and quick. Try *bekrí mezé* – lamb wrapped in vine leaves. €€

Nikola's Taverna, Agía Ánna Beach (after Platýs Gialós; no phone). A locals' favourite: an authentic Greek taverna on a tiny, pretty beach. €

Náfplio

Koutoúki to Parelthón, Profítis Ilías 12; tel: 275 202 9930. Excellent *mezédes* in an old building in the new town; outdoor eating in summer, and good prices. €€

Ómorfi Póli, Kotsonopoúlou 1; tel: 275 202 5944. Greek casseroles and grills with a twist; large portions. Book in advance as seating is limited. €€

Náxos

Gorgona, Agía Ánna (no phone). This

long-time beach taverna has grown more elaborate, but prices are still good, as is the traditional food. Try the *kakaviá* (fish stew). Locals eat here year-round. €€

Meltemi Restaurant, southern end of Hóra waterfront (no phone). The Meltemi has been here for 50 years, serving inexpensive Greek food, including fish. It's authentic and popular with locals. €

Páros

O Christos, opposite Panagía Pantanássa church, Naoússa; tel: 228 405 1442. One of Paros' most elegant restaurants; Mediterranean food, perfect service; expensive but excellent. €€€

Porphyra, Parikía; tel: 228 402 3410. Good fresh fish and shellfish; daily specialities include sea-urchin salad. €€

Rhodes

O Giannis, Vassiléos Georgíou tou Deftérou 23, Koskinoú (no phone). Abundant *mezédes*, washed down with Émbona wine or *oúzo*; extremely reasonable prices; dinner only. €

Ta Marasia, Agíou Ioánnou 155, southwest of Rhodes Old Town; tel: 224 103 4529. Currently the best *ouzerí* in Rhodes. The food's excellent if not very traditional – red cabbage, yoghurt with nuts, grilled oyster mushrooms – plus sea urchins and herring salad. €€

Mavrikos, Líndos; tel: 224 403 1232. Founded in 1933 and in the same family ever since, Mavrikos has been nominated one of the five best Greek eateries outside of Athens. *Mezédes* like *manoúri* cheese with basil and pine-nuts are accomplished, as are quasi-French main courses such as cuttlefish in wine sauce. €€

Sámos

Iy Psarades, Ágios Nikólaos Kondakeïkon; tel: 227 303 2489. Long reckoned the best fish taverna on the island, at surprisingly reasonable prices, plus the usual *orektiká*. €€

Kalypso, Mykáli beach; tel: 227 302 5198. Arguably the best beachfront taverna in the east of the island, with a good balance of seafood, salads and *magirevtá*. €€

To Kyma, east end of quay, Ágios Konstandínos (no phone). Good fried *mezédes*, barrel wine and various *magirevtá* make this a winner. €

Santorini

Sphinx, Firá; tel: 228 602 3823. Everything here is home-made, from the bread to the noodles. Try squid in basil sauce, and don't forget the chocolate soufflé. Expensive, but worth it for the food and the caldera view. €€€

Taverna Katina, Ammoúdi, Ía (no phone). On the right at the bottom of the steps leading down from Ía. Fresh, grilled fish, prawns, local specialities and excellent, friendly service make this the island's best taverna. €€

Taverna Pyrgos, Pýrgos Village (no phone). An elegant, moderately-priced restaurant with a view. Order a table full of their excellent *mezédes*, and don't miss the smoky aubergine salad. €€

Thessaloníki

Ta Adelfia tis Pyxarias, Platía Navarínou 7; tel: 231 026 6432. One of the best of several tavernas around a pedestrianised square east of the city centre. Succulent kebabs as well as a range of ready-made, oven-cooked dishes. €€

Amanites, D. Poliorkitoú 44; tel: 231 023 3513. A non-touristy place in the Kástra district that will appeal to vegetarians and carnivores alike. Features mushrooms *(amanítes)*, as well as a selection of meaty *mezédes*. €

To Yedi, I. Paparéska 13, Kastra; tel: 231 024 6495. Next to the Eptapýrgio fortress, this laid-back and friendly *ouzerí* does what *ouzerís* do best – no-nonsense high quality *mezédes* in a friendly, unfussy environment. House speciality is veal and aubergines served piping hot in a clay pot. €

ACTIVE HOLIDAYS

WATERSPORTS

With a coastline of 15,000km (9,300 miles), wind-surfing and sea-kayaking (especially along the south coast of Crete) are popular pursuits. Paragliding has pretty well replaced water-skiing for those who want to be towed. Wide sandy beaches proliferate on the west coast of the Peloponnese, in the east near Mount Olympus and also on the Halkidikí Peninsula. Snorkelling is permitted anywhere, and the rocky coastline is ideal.

Scuba diving is tightly controlled. in Greece. Many amateur divers have displeased the authorities by making off with ancient 'souvenirs' from the sea bed. If you are found diving in an unauthorised area, your tanks and gear will probably be confiscated and you may face prosecution. However, diving centres and schools exist in various areas where the archeological *eforía* or inspectorate has been placated. Popular spots where schools operate consistently include Halkidikí, Mýkonos, Rhodes, Ídra, Léros, Corfu and Crete.

SAILING

The Aegean Sea is the perfect place for sailors. Numerous companies offer sailing packages and cruises around the coast of Greece that can be booked from home. Much of the sailing is in flotillas helmed by skippers furnished by charter companies, but experienced sailors can charter their own yacht. Alternatively, once you're in Greece you can hire boats by the day or week at many marinas.

The best times to sail are spring and autumn, as winds can be high in summer and prices are hiked up to many times those of the cooler seasons.

There are schools housed in the *navtikí ómili* (sailing clubs) of the following cities: Athens (Paleó Fáliro); Thessaloníki; Corfu; Vólos; Rhodes; Sámos; Híos; Sýros; Kalamáta; Alexandroúpolis. Further information available from the Hellenic Yachting Federation, 7 Aktí Navárhou Koundourióti, Piraeus, tel: 210 413 7531, fax: 210 413 1119.

HIKING AND WINTER SPORTS

Hikers, hill-walkers and mountaineers are spoilt for choice in Greece. Try an ascent of the country's highest peak, Mount Olympus *(see page 77)*, traverse the huge Víkos Gorge *(see page 65)* or go walking on the Pílion Peninsula *(see page 79)*. The best, detailed topographical maps to the back country, at scales of about 1:50,000, are produced by two rival companies: Road Editions and Anavasi. Between them they cover all the mainland mountain ranges and quite a number of the more hikeable islands in the Sporádes and Cyclades.

Although Greek snow conditions will never rival the Alps, there are plenty of ski centres in the mountains, that are loved by the Greeks. Mt Párnassos has name recognition and Mt Veloúhi is also conveniently close to Athens, but the best ski centres are in the north, on Mt Vérmio and Mt Kaïmáktsalan. Peloponnesians make do with the small resort on Mt Hélmos.

Spectator sports

Football is the main spectator sport, with matches played on Wednesday and Sunday afternoons. Top teams include AEK and Panathinaïkós of Athens, Olympiakós of Pireaus, and PAOK of Thessaloníki — and of course the national side, which stunned everyone with their victory in the 2004 European championships. Football is run a close second by basketball. For matches, check local papers.

PRACTICAL INFORMATION

Getting There

BY AIR

Greece is served by numerous international airlines. Charter flights arrive
from mid-April to late October. Sched-
uled airlines flying direct from the UK
include Olympic, BA, Hellas Jet and
easyJet; from the US the only direct
services are on Olympic and Delta.

Eleftherios Venizelos International
Airport in Spáta, some 25km (15
miles) northeast of central Athens,
opened in March 2001. A ring road
called the Attikí Odós has been constructed around the northern suburbs,
linking the airport area with Elefsína.
A light-rail extension runs between the
last metro station of Doukíssis Plakendías and the airport, but is expensive
(€8 for one person, €12 for two travelling together), so the express buses
remain popular. No E94 goes every 15
minutes to the Ethnikí Ámyna stop of
the metro, while No E95 goes every 20
minutes to Sýndagma Square, and No
E96 every 20 minutes to Karaïskaki
Square in Piraeus, via Korópi and the
coastal suburbs. There are other less
frequent E-lines to Dáfni metro station, Kifissiá and the Kifissoú bus station. All services run around the clock
(much less frequently 11pm–5am) and
cost €2.90, which also gives you the
run of Athens public transport for 24
hours from the start time of the ticket.

BY SEA

Most visitors going to Greece by sea
do so from Italy. You can get a boat
to Greece from Venice, Trieste,
Ancona and Bari, but the most regular
and quickest service is from Brindisi.
Daily ferry lines (somewhat less frequent in low season) connect Brindisi
with the three main western Greek
ports: Corfu, Igoumenítsa and Pátra.

Corfu is a maximum 9-hour trip;
Igoumenítsa 11 hours; and Pátra 16–
18 hours, depending on whether you
take a direct boat or one that makes
stops in Corfu and Igoumenítsa. The
use of 'Superfast' ferries, where available, will cut crossing times by a good
25 percent.

Igoumenítsa is the ideal port of call
for those setting off to central or western Greece. Pátra is best if you want to
head directly to Athens or into the
Peloponnese; it's possible to stop-over
at little or no extra charge on Corfu
before continuing to Igoumenítsa or
Pátra if you specify this at the outset.
Regular buses and trains connect Pátra
and Athens (3–4 hours).

At present there are no services
from Croatia or Montenegro to
Greece, nor are there passenger links
with Egypt or Israel. Once a week
there is a service from Cyprus (Limas-
sol), calling at Rhodes and Piraeus.
There are also connections between
the Dodecanese and northeast Aegean
islands and the corresponding ports on
the Turkish coast; the most regular and
affordable are Lésvos–Ayvalık,
Sámos–Kusadası and Híos–Çesme.

OVERLAND

The overland route from northwestern
Europe to Greece is a long one, some
3,000km (1,900 miles) from London
to Athens. Since troubles in former
Yugoslavia, and the advent of no-frills
airlines, there is no longer a through
bus service between Greece and the
UK, always a miserable three-and-a-
half-day trip at the best of times. If you
don't want to fly, the most cost-effec-
tive way to get to Greece is to buy an
Interrail pass that includes the Adriatic
ferry crossing, and make the land journey through France and Italy to the
port of choice. It is in theory possible

to go overland through Hungary, Romania and Bulgaria, to Thessaloníki in northern Greece. Car drivers will probably opt for the motorway through France and Italy and then an Adriatic ferry.

Getting Around

BY CAR

Driving etiquette in Greece is very different from northwestern Europe. Practices such as tailgating, barging out of side-roads without stopping, and overtaking on the right are common practice. Drivers rarely keep to speed limits (100kmph/62mph on motorways, 80kmph/50mph outside towns, 50kmph/31mph in towns).

The road network is dense but of variable quality; many roads that start off with good surfaces and markings may end up as rough tracks. Road signs show places in both Greek and Latin scripts. Visitors will find the few existing toll-motorways well worth using; the main stretches are Athens–Thessaloníki, Athens–Pátra, and the steadily lengthening Via Egnatia that will eventually cross Epirus, Macedonia and Thrace between Igoumenítsa and the Turkish border.

Hiring a car costs €25–50 a day depending on the season, while a 50cc scooter (*papáki*) costs €10–16 a day. Seat belts and helmets must be worn. Full insurance cover is recommended.

BY BUS

Most villages can be reached by bus, although there are fewer services than formerly. The old green-and-white KTEL buses are being supplanted on the most popular routes by midnight-blue-and-aquamarine models with special steps for people with disabilities. Buses are strictly non-smoking. Departure times are given at ticket windows, where you buy tickets before boarding; fares are reasonable.

Many towns have more than one bus station. In Athens, buses to the Peloponnese and Thessaloníki leave from the Kifissoú terminal. Catch the blue No 51 from the corner of Zínonos and Menándrou (near Omónia). Delphi, Metéora and Vólos are served by buses from the Liossíon station, which can be reached by the blue No 24 from Eleisthériou Venizélou. In Thessaloníki buses to Athens and Ioánnina leave from Monastiríou 67 (near the station), although a unified station has been set up in the Sfagiá district, and most services are eventually supposed to start from there.

> **By Taxi**
> Using taxis to get to rural destinations can be expensive, unless you share. In cities, taxis are affordable as long as you get an honest driver who 'zeroes' the meter at the outset. In Athens, shared taxis are the rule – you pay the difference in meter reading between getting in and alighting, subject to a minimum fare. Urban taxi-drivers are not obliged to take passengers, and will only do so if your destination suits them.

BY TRAIN

Greek railways are a delight if one enjoys travelling for its own sake, but often frustrating if speed and efficiency are more important. It is worth travelling first class, which is only slightly more expensive.

A rail circuit of the Peloponnese, via Árgos, Trípoli, Kalamáta, the west coast, Pátra and Corinth, is reasonably priced, although the line is ancient and locomotives slow (except between Athens and Pátra). The Vólos–Kalambáka was widened to standard gauge in 2001. The showcase Intercity train from Athens to Thessaloníki takes about six hours, but services beyond, towards Turkey, are antiquated and neglected. There are two stations in Athens: Lárissa serves northern Greece and has its own metro station (Stathmós Laríssis). The Peloponnese station is accessible via a pedestrian overpass from Stathmós Laríssis.

BY BOAT

Most of the Aegean islands can be reached from Piraeus, but there are also services from Rafína and Lávrio on the east Attic coast. The Sporádes are best served from Vólos; and Thessaloníki, Kavála and Alexandroúpoli in northern Greece also have frequent services. The weather is a major factor; winds above Force 7–8 result in cancellations. Craft range from old rust-buckets to sleek new catamarans and high speed craft. Catamarans have mostly eclipsed the Flying Dolphin hydrofoils, but a few of these still operate in the north Dodecanese, and remain the most popular way to reach the Argo-Saronic islands (from Aktí Tzelépi in Piraeus). Outside peak season you can buy a ticket from quayside agencies the same day – they are

no longer sold on board. Ferry schedules can be obtained from the Greek National Tourist Office *(see page 119)*. Timetables are online at: www.ferries.gr and www.gtpnet.com.

BY PLANE

Many of the islands are served from Athens and Thessaloníki by Olympic Airlines or its subsidiary Olympic Aviation, but the state monopoly has been broken by Aegean Air on busy lines such as Athens–Crete and Athens–Rhodes. There are also some useful radial routes, such as Rhodes-Sámos–Híos–Lésvos–Límnos–Thessaloníki; and Corfu–Préveza–Kefalloniá–Zákynthos.

IN ATHENS

The smart, newish Athens Metro (daily 5am–midnight) incorporates the old Line 1, from Piraeus to Kifissiá, Line 2 (Ágios Dimítrios to Ágios Andónios) and Line 3 (Monastiráki to Doukíssis Plakendías). A day-pass is the most economical way to travel. Summer 2004 saw the addition of three tram lines: Néos Kósmos metro station to Ágios Kosmás, Glyfáda to

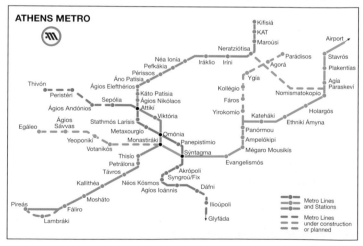

Néo Fáliro, and Sýndagma to Glyfáda. Sleek new buses and trolleys go virtually everywhere else (5am–midnight); bus lanes have helped speed them up, and there are express routes prefixed X or Z. Tickets are sold in books of 10, from newagent kiosks and booths at bus and metro stations.

Facts for the Visitor

TRAVEL DOCUMENTS
With a valid passport, citizens of the European Union/European Economic Area, the United States, Canada, Australia and New Zealand can enter Greece and stay for up to three months as tourists. No visa is necessary. Fines for overstaying this period are heavy.

CUSTOMS
Visitors from EU countries may bring in and take out goods for personal use. Restrictions apply to non-EU citizens and there are also limits on what may be exported duty-free. The export of antiques is forbidden.

TOURIST INFORMATION
The Greek National Tourist Organisation is known as the GNTO, or EOT. **In the UK: Greek National Tourist Organisation**, 4 Conduit Street, London W1R 0DJ, tel: (020) 7734 5997. **In the US:** Head Office, Olympic Tower, 645 Fifth Ave., 5th Floor, New York 10022, tel: (212) 421 5777. **In Athens:** 26 Amalías, tel. 210 331 0392. There are EOT offices in the larger Greek towns such as Mytilíni, Haniá, Pátra, etc. Typical opening times are Mon–Fri 8am–2.30pm, sometimes longer in high summer, when they may also open at weekends.

The Tourist Police are not an information source, except in emergencies *(see box)*; otherwise they are there to receive complaints about hotel or taverna rip-offs.

CURRENCY AND EXCHANGE
The Greek unit of currency is the euro, though the equivalent in drachmas is still often quoted on till receipts (€1 euro = approx. 340 drachmes). There are ATMs in all major towns and resorts; they accept most credit and debit cards. Travellers' cheques are not much used any more and can only be exchanged at bank counters. Credit cards are useful for buying domestic air tickets and as a deposit for car hire, but less useful in all but the flashiest tavernas, and ferry agents may levy a 3 percent commission on their use.

Emergencies
Police, tel: 100
Ambulance, tel: 166
Fire brigade, tel: 199.
The Tourist Police HQ number is 210 171 (24 hours). They should speak English and have information about hospitals with emergency facilities. For roadside assistance contact the ELPA motoring organisation, tel: 10400, if you belong to an affiliate auto club overseas.

OPENING TIMES
Most shops open Mon, Wed and Sat 8.30am–2.30pm; Tues, Thur and Fri 8.30am–2pm and 5.30–8.30pm. Post offices open Mon–Fri 7.30am–2pm; banks open Mon–Thur 8am–2.30pm, Fri 8am–2pm. Minor, state-controlled archaeological sites and museums, usually open Tues–Sun 8.30am–3pm; major attractions may adhere to this schedule in off-season, but keep longer hours (8am–7pm) in summer. National museums and archeological sites are usually free on Sunday in off-season; otherwise charges range from €2 (minor provincial sites) to €8 (the Acropolis).

PUBLIC HOLIDAYS

The official public holidays are: 1 January (*Protokhroniá*); 6 January (Epiphany/*Theofánia*); 25 March (Independence Day/*Evangelismós*); Good Friday/*Megáli Paraskeví*; Easter/*Páskha* (variable); 1 May (Labour Day/*Protomagiá*); Pentecost/*Áyio Pnévma*; 15 August (*Kímisis tis Theotókou*/Dormition of the Virgin); 28 October (Óhi Day); 25 December (Christmas/*Hristoúgena*); 26 December (*Sýnaxis tis Panayías*/ Gathering of the Virgin's Entourage).

Time
Greece is on Eastern European Time which is two hours ahead of GMT, seven hours ahead of Eastern Standard Time.

PERIPTERA

Every Greek village has a pavement kiosk or *períptero*. These often stay open until after midnight and supply everyday items ranging from newspapers to sweets and aspirins, as well as top-up cards for mobile phones.

POSTAL SERVICES

Postboxes are yellow for ordinary services, red for express. *Esoterikó* = inland and *exoterikó* = overseas. Post offices (*tahydromía*) are recognisable by their logo, a stylised Hermes-head on a blue background. Stamps *(grammatósima)* can be bought at post offices or in stationers' *(hartopolía)*. Postal rates are subject to fairly frequent change. If sending a parcel anywhere outside the EU/EEA, don't seal it until a post office clerk has inspected it. Letters can be sent *post restante* to any main post office. Take your passport when you go to pick up mail.

TELEPHONES

Public phone boxes are card-operated and cards may be obtained from kiosks. There are two kinds: simple *telekártes* and the more economical *khronokártes*. Most people, however, rely on mobile phones. If you bring your own handset from overseas, don't make the mistake of 'roaming' and incurring the horrendous charges (typically £0.70/€1.05 per minute, plus VAT). Make sure your phone is unblocked to accept other SIMs before you leave home then buy a Greek pay-as-you-go SIM card from one of the four networks. This will pay for itself within a few days.

CLOTHING

Stony paths and uneven, cobbled or marble-slab streets demand sturdy footwear. Shorts, trousers on women, and sleeveless T-shirts on either sex are forbidden in monasteries and churches. Away from tourist resorts it is best to dress modestly.

SUNBATHING AND BEACHES

Nude sunbathing is forbidden except on certain designated beaches, but if you're hidden from public view it should be all right. Visitors should respect the sensitivities of the local people, particularly older ones, who can be upset by such behaviour, even if they do not show it. Attitudes are changing towards topless sunbathing and on many beaches in the popular resorts it has become acceptable. In accordance with Greek law, beaches are public places and hotels or sunbed concessions are not allowed to completely block admission to their particular strip, although there are various ways to discourage you strolling in.

TOILETS

Public toilets, usually subterranean in a central park, vary in cleanliness. It's not done to use the loos in a café or bar without buying a drink – signs to that effect may remind you of this.

CHURCHES AND MONASTERIES

In churches and monasteries, women should cover their shoulders and knees and men should not wear shorts. It is also considered rude to cross your legs or stand with your hands behind your back. Churches are normally closed if there is no attendant present. Ask at a nearby bar or café if the key is available (avoid the siesta period). Key-holders do not generally expect a tip, but always leave a generous offering in the church money box.

NEWSPAPERS

British papers usually arrive in Greece a day late, although may be available the same afternoon in Athens. The *Athens News* is an English language weekly (every Friday), with worthwhile events and cinema listings.

MEDICAL ASSISTANCE

The Greek word for doctor is *iatrós* and a dentist is *odondíatros*. Many Greek doctors have studied abroad and speak at least one foreign language, often English. Greece has a reciprocal health agreement with the rest of the EU, which means visitors are entitled to treatment under the Greek National Health scheme; E111 forms are rarely asked for. Where there isn't a state hospital *(kratikó nosokomío)*, there will be an *agrotikó iatrío* (rural clinic) where basic treatment is free.

Chemists *(farmakía)* are identified by a green cross. They only work morning hours Mon–Fri, but there is always one after-hours duty pharmacist in a neighbourhood or village (a bilingual English/Greek rota is posted on the door of closed chemists).

DIPLOMATIC REPRESENTATION

UK: Ploutárhou 1, Athens, tel: 210 723 6211.
USA: Vassilísis Sofías 91, Athens, tel: 210 721 2951.

SECURITY AND CRIME

Greece is one of the safest countries in Europe. Rates of crime against people are low, although petty theft and burglary (especially car break-ins) are on the rise.

WOMEN TRAVELLERS

Women visitors to Greece will experience no more hassle than in Italy or Spain – possibly less. Social mores have changed greatly since the 1970s and the local lothario cruising for foreign women is virtually extinct. In less touristy areas, however, rural Greeks are highly traditional and may find it hard to understand why you are alone. You may also find drinking in all-male *kafenía* a bit uncomfortable.

CHILDREN

Children are adored and indulged, but not allowed to run roughshod over adult schedules. They are inculcated early into the rhythm of late-night taverna meals. For family holidays, beaches on the Halkidikí Peninsula, the larger Cyclades like Páros and Náxos, and the southwestern Peloponnese have wonderful sand.

ELECTRICITY

220 volts out of round-pin sockets; bring adaptors for UK appliances. US visitors should bring transformers for 110-volt items.

Photography

It is usual for photographers to be asked to pay a supplement for using cameras in museums, and the use of tripods and video cameras is forbidden. Photography of any kind is not normally permitted in churches. Photographs of museum exhibits are available on request from the Archaeological Receipts Fund, 57 Panepistimou, Athens, tel: 210 325 3901.

ACCOMMODATION

Enikiazómena domátia – rented rooms – can be found in most islands and coastal resorts. Most such rooms are good value, and nowadays tend to be actual studios with their own facilities. Proprietors touting at the port is on the wane, but still far from unknown; if you go with one, you are not obliged to take the room (and it is best to avoid unlicensed premises).

Rented rooms have to close down between October and Easter, when you have to patronise those hotels that remain open. Breakfast will be available in all establishments of C-class and above *(see box)*. Mainland hotels can be poor value, except in places like Delfí and Meteóra where stiff competition dictates realistic pricing. Hotels near any ski resort will of course have their high season at winter weekends rather than in summer.

There is a growing number of boutique hotels and inns, often in restored buildings of historical interest. The biggest concentrations are in Rhodes Old Town, Crete, the Cyclades, Mt Pílio, Zagória and the Máni. All are now in private hands, since the EOT (Greek National Tourist Board) relinquished their interest in such projects.

Camp sites are situated mainly on Halkidikí, on the coasts of Epirus (west) and the Thermaic Gulf (east), on the Peloponnese, Crete and around Meteóra or Delphi. Rough camping is forbidden, although it is the rule when trekking in the high mountains.

Hotel Selection

The following hotels are divided into three categories: €€€ = expensive; €€ = moderate; €= inexpensive.

Aegina

Hotel Brown, Aegina Town;tel: 229 702 2271, fax: 229 702 5838, brownhotel @aig.forthnet.gr. Set on the southern waterfront a 5-minute walk from the ferry quay this hotel is still owned by the original partly-English family (hence the name). Rooms are spacious and tidy and there's a large leafy garden. €€

Athens

Grande Bretagne, Sýndagma Square; tel: 210 333 0000, fax: 210 332 8034, www.grandebretagne.gr. Expensive and plush, the Grande Bretagne is the doyen of Athenian hotels. This historic building oozes class, from its luxurious rooms, to its beautiful spa. €€€

St George Lycabettus, Kleoménous 2, Kolonáki; tel: 210 729 0711, fax: 210 729 0439, www.sglycabettus.gr. Recently renovated and now styling itself a boutique hotel. The cool, comfortable rooms and suites are elegant, and the rooftop pool is a delight. Two good restaurants, one with a view over the Acropolis. €€€

Museum, Bouboulínas 16 and Tosítsa; tel: 210 380 5611, fax: 210 380 0507, www.bestwestern.com. This well-run hotel is close to the Archaeological Museum. Rooms are plain and comfortable, but a little over-priced. No restaurant but breakfast is included. €€

Acropolis View, Webster 10 and Robértou Gáli; tel: 210 921 7303, www.acrop-

---

Hotel classification

Hotels are checked by the Greek National Tourist Organisation (EOT); they are placed in a total of six categories – L (luxury) and A to E. Each hotel is classified according to the amenities on offer. Prices are fixed for each category, although the category does not give much indication of the quality of the room. Town hotels, especially on the mainland, are generally about 20 percent more expensive than those in the country.

olisview.gr. The view of the Acropolis is from only a few of the 32 rooms. Rooms are small but clean and well-cared-for, and the hotel has had a makeover. Excellent location, with nearby metro. €€

Attalos, Athinás 29; tel: 210 321 2801–3, fax: 210 324 3124, www.attalos.gr. Fairly standard but comfortable rooms close to Monastiráki Square (noisy in the day but quietens down at night). Staff are attentive and friendly; fine view of the city and the Acropolis from the roof terrace. €

Aphrodite, Einárdou 12 and M. Vóda 65; tel: 210 881 0589/210 881 6574, www.hostelaphrodite.com. Clean, unpretentious and friendly, this small hotel is a good deal. Slightly off the beaten track but midway between Viktoria and Stathmós Lárisas metro stations. C

Marble House, A. Zínni 35, Koukáki; tel: 210 922 8294/923 4058, fax: 210 922 6461, www.marblehouse.gr. This inexpensive, clean and friendly hotel may be the best deal in Athens, conveniently close to the Syngroú-Fix metro. Some rooms have air-conditioning (the others have powerful ceiling fans). It has been done up recently and prices remain low for the city. €

Corfu

Bella Venezia, Napoleóntos Zambéli 4, Kérkyra Town; tel: 266 104 6500/20708, belvnht@hol.gr. Neoclassical mansion well adapted as a B-class hotel in a central yet quiet location to the south of the old town. €€

Konstantinoupolis, Zavitsiánou 11, Old Port, Kérkyra Town; tel: 266 104 8716, fax: 266 104 8718, polis@ker.forthnet.gr. 1862 building, once a backpackers' hostel, now lovingly restored as a well-priced C-class hotel with sea and mountain views. Comfortable rooms and common areas, lift. €€

Nefeli, Komméno, Kérkyra Town; tel: 266 109 1033, fax: 266 109 0290. This small inland hotel in mock Neoclassical style, spread over three buildings among olive groves, has a loyal clientele, good service and air-conditioning. €€

Palace Mon Repos, Anemómylos district, Garítsa Bay; tel: 266 103 2783, fax: 266 102 3459. Renovated in the late 1990s, this hotel is the closest thing Kérkyra Town has to a beach resort. Views to the sea, Old Fort and Mon Repos woods, and a small swimming pool. €€

Pelekas Country Club, Km 8 Kérkyra –Pélekas road; tel: 266 105 2239, fax: 266 105 2919, reservations@country-club.gr. Corfu's most exclusive rural hotel, 26 units in an 18th-century mansion set in landscaped grounds. Stylish breakfasts in the central refectory, pool, tennis, helipad. €€€

Casa Lucia, Sgómbou hamlet, Km 12 of Kérkyra–Paleokastrítsa road; tel: 266 109 1419, fax: 266 109 1732, caslucia@otenet.gr. Peaceful setting at centre of the island. A restored olive-mill complex set among lovingly tended gardens comprises 11 units ranging from studios to family cottages. Most have kitchens, all share a large pool. €€

Levant Hotel, above Pélekas, beside Kaiser's Throne; tel: 266 109 4230, fax: 266 109 4115, www.levant-hotel.com. 1990s-built hotel in mock-traditional style, with superb views over the island. Rooms are wood-floored, baths marble-trimmed; small pool, and some great beaches a few kilometers away. €€

Liapades Beach Hotel, Liapádes; tel: 066 304 1294. Two smallish wings make up this amiable C-class at one of the quieter beach resorts on this coast. €€

Crete

Lato Hotel, Amoúdi; tel: 284 102 4581, fax: 284 102 3996, lato@mail.com. On the beach, 1 km (½ mile) from Ágios Nikolaos, with 37 rooms set in lush gardens. They also manage the Karavostasi on the coast 8 km (5 miles) from town, with three self-catering studios. €€

Elounda Beach Hotel, Elounda; tel: 284 104 1812, fax: 284 104 1373, www. eloundabeach.gr. Regarded as one of the island's best. Fabulously expensive but exceptionally luxurious – some of the suites have a private pool, sauna and gym. And, of course, helicopter transfer is laid on as well. €€€

Casa Delfino Suites, Theofánous 9, near Zambelíou, Haniá; tel: 282 109 3098, fax: 282 109 6500, www.casadel fino.com. Beautifully restored 17th-century Venetian house in the old harbour area; 20 luxury apartments around a courtyard. €€€

Contessa,Theofánous 15, near Zambelíou, Haniá, tel/fax: 282 109 8565. Spacious rooms in a fine Venetian building, with expensive furniture, wooden floors and ceilings. €€

Kastro Hotel, Theotokopoúlou 22, Iráklio; tel: 281 028 4185, fax: 281 022 3622, www.kastro-hotel.gr. Comfortable, medium-sized hotel with a great roof-terrace for sunbathing; spacious rooms. €€

Lato Hotel, Epimenídou 15, Iráklio; tel: 281 022 8103, fax: 281 024 0350, www.lato.gr. Family-run hotel overlooking Venetian fortress on old harbour. €€

Dimitsána

Xenonas Kazakou, tel/fax: 279 503 1660. A traditional guesthouse in an attractively restored stone house, towards the top of the village. €

Évia (Euboa)

Hotel Karystion, Kriezótou 2, Kárystos; tel: 222 402 2391, fax: 222 402 2727. A busy, friendly hotel in the far south of Évia, close to the fortress. Air-conditioned rooms, with balconies, TVs and phones. Good bathing spots a few minutes' walk way. €€

Híos

Kyma, east end of Evgenías Handrí; tel: 227 104 4500, fax: 227 104 4600. B-class hotel in a converted Neoclassical

mansion (plus less attractive modern extension); helpful management, good breakfasts in the original salon. €€

Mavrokordatiko, Kámbos district, Mitaráki lane; tel: 227 103 2900, www.mavro kordatiko.com. The best and most popular of the restoration projects in the Kámbos, with heated, wood-panelled rooms and breakfast (included) served by the courtyard with its *mánganos* (waterwheel). €€

Hydra (Ídra)

Miranda, Ídra Town; tel: 229 805 2230, fax: 229 805 3510. Set in an 1810 mansio, Miranda is a traditional style hotel with 14 differently decorated rooms, some traditional in style, others art deco. Classy atmosphere is enhanced by the in-house art gallery. Breakfast served in the garden. €€

Kalamáta

Iviskos Hotel, Fáron 196; tel: 272 106 2511, fax 272 108 2323. Set in a lovingly cared-for Neoclassical building. €

Kastoriá

Eolís, Agíou Athanasíou 30; tel: 246 702 1070.Close to town centre, a delightful restored mansion, once a consulate. A neat boutique hotel, with lavishly furnished rooms and all mod cons. €€

Kórinthos

Ephira, Ethnikís Andistásis 52; tel: 274 102 2434, fax: 274 102 4514, www.ephi rahotel.gr. A pleasant modern hotel, well-priced and very near the bus station and the centre of town. Internal rooms have less traffic noise. €

Lésvos

Pension Lida, Plomári; tel/fax: 225 203 2507. Welcoming inn in two adjacent old mansions formerly belonging to a soap-manufacturing magnate; sea-view balconies for most units, enthusiastic management. €€

Monmvasía

Lazareto, tel: 273 206 1991, fax: 273 206 1992, lazaretohotel@yahoo.com. At the foot of the Monemvasiá rock, overlooking the causeway, the stone-walled ruins of the old hospital have been converted into a discreetly luxurious hotel with a good restaurant. €€€

Mycenae

La Belle Hélène, tel: 275 107 6225, fax: 275 107 6179. Reasonable prices, and with the feel of an English country B&B, as conservation rules mean no en-suite bathrooms. Attached restaurant has guestbook with celebrity signatures. (The archaelogist Schliemann lived here while excavating Mycenae.) €€

Mýkonos

Deliades, Ornós; tel: 228 907 9430, fax: 228 902 6996, www.hoteldeliadesmykonos.com. Built in 2001 with quiet taste, a short walk up the hill from Ornós beach. Every room has a big terrace with sea view. Relaxed atmosphere, pool, port and airport transfer. €€
Myconian Inn, Hóra; tel: 228 902 3420, fax: 228 902 7269, mycinn@hotmail.com. Right on the upper edge of town, this hotel is convenient, quiet, unpretentious and tasteful. Balconies overlook the port. €

Náfpaktos

Aktí, Grímbovo; tel: 263 402 8464, fax: 263 402 4171, akti@otenet.gr. This is the town's clear winner, set behind the easterly beach. The breakfast is of a good standard, and top-floor suites are palatial. €€

Náfplio

Nafplio Palace, Akronavplía; tel: 275 207 0800, fax: 275 202 8783, www.nafplionhotels.gr. Low-key but luxurious, set inside the walls of the Akronavplía fortress, and with fabulous views out across the sea to Boúrtzi island. €€€
Marianna Pension,Potamaníou 9; tel:

275 202 4256, fax: 275 209 9365, www.pensionmarianna.gr. A beautifully refurbished pension, tucked under the walls of the Akronavplía fortress. Breakfast terrace has wonderful views. €€

Náxos

Chateau Zevgoli, Hóra;tel: 228 502 2993, fax: 228 502 5200, chateau-zevgoli@nax.forthnet.gr. Quiet, plush and exclusive, high up in the old town. A Venetian mansion with only 10 rooms, each lovingly decorated. One has a four-poster bed, most have great views. €€

Neos Mystrás

Vyzantion; tel: 273 108 3309, fax: 273 102 0019, byzanhtl@otenet.gr.Recently refurbished hotel; most bathrooms have full-sized tubs, most rooms an unbeatable view of the Byzantine ruins. €€

Olymbía (Olympia)

Hercules; tel: 262 402 2696, fax: 262 402 2213. Quiet location near the church, with welcoming management. €€

Páros

Pandrossos Hotel, Parikía; tel: 228 402 1394, fax: 228 402 3501, www.pandrossoshotel.gr. On a pretty hill at Parikia's edge, yet in town. Beautiful views of the bay, pool, good restaurant, marble lobby. €€
Dina, Parikía; tel: 228 402 1325, fax: 228 402 3525. Friendly hotel in the heart of the old town. Spotlessly clean rooms set around a lovely flowered courtyard. Only 8 rooms, so book early. €

Póros

Hotel Manessi, Póros Town; tel: 229 802 2273, fax: 229 802 4345, manessis@otenet.gr. A pleasant waterfront choice right in the centre. Housed in a Neoclassical building all rooms are well equipped with central heating and air-conditioning, TV and fridge and most have balconies looking over the port. €

Seven Brothers Hotel, Platía Iróön, Póros Town; tel: 229 802 3412, fax: 229 802 3413, www.poros.com.gr/ 7brothers. A small family-run hotel with a restaurant. Rooms are large and comfortable, with TV and air-conditioning. Very handy for centre of Póros Town and the ferry and hydrofoil quay. €€

Rhodes
Andréas Hotel, Omírou 28d, Old Town; tel: 224 103 4156, fax: 224 107 4285, www.hotelandreas.com. An old favourite under dynamic new management, this pension in an old Turkish mansion was refurbished in 2003. En-suite rooms, terrace bar, excellent breakfasts; minimum two-night stay. €€
Ganymedes, Perikléous 68, Rhodes Old Town; tel: 224 107 8631, fax: 224 107 8632, www.hotel-ganymedes.com. Just four rooms at this 2003-built boutique hotel, three large and airy, one best as a single, all exquisitely furnished. There's a roof terrace for evenings, and a French patisserie on the ground floor. €€
Niki's, Sofokléous 39, Rhodes Old Town; tel: 224 102 5115, fax: 224 103 6033. An excellent budget hotel; most of the rooms have air-conditioning and balconies. Helpful management. €

Sámos
Aïdonokastro, Platanáki/Aïdónia district, near Ágios Konstandínos; tel: 227 309 4686, fax: 227 309 4404. About half the abandoned hillside hamlet of Valeondádes has been renovated; each former house now a pair of two- or four-person units with traditional touches. €€
Amfilisos, Bállos beach, near Órmos Marathókambos; tel: 227 303 1669, fax: 227 303 1668. The hotel itself is nothing extraordinary, but Bállos is a deliciously sleepy place for doing very little except exploring the coast to the southeast and sampling some good local tavernas. €€
Avli Pension, Áreos 2, Sámos Town; tel: 227 302 2939. Housed in the former convent school of French nuns, this is the best budget choice in town. Just over half the rooms round the courtyard are en-suite. Affable owner Spyros is a reliable source of local information. €

Santorini
Fanari Villas, Ía; tel: 228 607 1008. Traditional *skaftá* cave houses converted into luxury accommodation. Pool, breakfast terrace, bar and 240 steps down to Ammoudiá Bay. Friendly service. €€€
Hermes, Kamári; tel: 228 603 1664, fax: 228 603 3240, www.hermeshotel-santorini.com. Friendly, family-run hotel set in beautiful gardens not far from town centre and the black beach. Pool, comfortable rooms, and all the amenities. €€

Sithonía
Villa Rena, Órmos Panagías, Ágios Nikólaos; tel: 037 531 989. Quiet family pension by the sea. Car and bike hire. €

Thessaloníki
Bristol Capsis, Oplopioú and Katoúni 2; tel: 231 050 6500, fax: 231 051 5777, www.capsishotel.gr. Thessaloníki's most sumptuous boutique hotel. Sixteen rooms each immaculately restored in the shell of the former Bristol Hotel. €€€
Electra Palace, Plateía Aristotélous 9; tel: 231 029 4000, fax: 231 029 4001, www.forthnet.gr/electrapalace. A central hotel, overlooking the broad Platía Aristotélous. Neoclassical facade, very imposing and very comfortable. €€€
Le Palace, Tsimiskí 12; tel: 231 025 7300, fax: 231 022 1270, www.lepalace.gr. Another central hotel in a 1920s building. Renovated in 2002, its style is reminiscent of Paris in the 1930s. €€
Mediterranean Palace, Salamínos and Karatásou; tel: 231 055 2554, fax: 231 055 2622, www.mediterranean-palace.gr. Very close to the port and Ladádika district. An imposing belle époque hotel; large, lavishly furnished rooms and light public areas. €€€

INDEX